12.95

Longman/Institute of Housing

The Housing Practice Series

D1180985

Housing Finance

Longman

INSTITUTE OF
HOUSING

David Garnett, Barbara Reid, Helen Riley

Published by the Institute of Housing (Services) Ltd, Units 15 and 16
Mercia Business Village, Westwood Business Park, Torwood Close,
Coventry CV4 8HX and Longman Group UK Ltd, 6th Floor,
Westgate House, The High, Harlow, Essex CM20 1YR

Tel (0279) 442601; Fax (0279) 444501

Published in the IOH/Longman Housing Practice Series under the General
Editorship of Peter Williams

© IOH (Services) Ltd & Longman Group UK Ltd 1990

All rights reserved. No part of this publication may be reproduced, stored in
a retrieval system, or transmitted in any form or by any means, electronic,
mechanical, photocopying, recording or otherwise, without either the prior
written permission of the Copyright owner of a licence permitting restricted
copying issued by the Copyright Licensing Agency Ltd, 33–34 Alfred Place,
London WC1E 1DP.

First published 1990

Reprinted 1990

British Library Cataloguing in Publication Data

Garnett, David
  Housing finance. – (Housing practice)
  1. Great Britain. Housing. Finance
  I. Title II. Reid, Barbara III. Riley, Helen, IV. Williams, Peter
  V. Series
  338.4'33635'0941

ISBN 0–582–02956–2

ISBN 0-582-02956-2

1034732   1

Typeset by Quorn Selective Repro Ltd, Loughborough, Leics.
Printed and bound in Great Britain by
Biddles Ltd, Guildford and King's Lynn

Contents

Contents

Preface

This book is directed at those who wish to acquire a straightforward and up-to-date overview of the system of housing finance. This means that it will be of real interest to all those who are currently working in the housing field as well as those who are seeking to work there whether in a professional, voluntary or political capacity. We have paid particular attention to the needs of that growing group of students on qualifying or exempting diploma and degree courses which lead to membership of the Institute of Housing, the Royal Institution of Chartered Surveyors and the Royal Town Planning Institute. The book will also be of interest to those following academic courses in social and public administration and to the general reader concerned with issues relating to the built environment and public affairs.

The text provides a mix of analysis and description: it is not intended to be a manual but an introduction and guide to the subject. It has been written at a time when government policy and legislation is subjecting the whole system of housing and housing finance to significant organisational and operational changes. In order to take these changes into account, the first two chapters identify the basic, underlying, unchanging nature and scope of the subject and point to some of the constant issues which surround it.

The first chapter begins with a brief consideration of housing as a commodity and emphasises that a proper understanding of housing finance is dependent upon a prior appreciation of the fact that housing as an artefact simultaneously possesses consumption, investment and social characteristics. It goes on to outline a simple cross-tenure, functional analysis of the system of housing finance which makes the point that financial resources are a means to an end rather than an end in themselves. It stresses that, in the final analysis, it is *how finance is used* rather than what finance is that is of consequence. The first chapter also introduces the reader to some basic financial and accounting concepts and terms. The second chapter places the subject of housing finance in its wider political, social and economic context.

In writing this book, a conscious effort has been made to provide the reader with a simple and clear conceptual framework with which to approach the subject's constantly changing detail. This 'organising frame' is based on what can be termed a *functional analysis* of housing finance. From the start, it is argued that housing finance should be understood to have two broad functions: to *provide* housing and to *manage* housing once it has been provided. (Income support is treated as a welfare finance rather than as a housing finance function). These two broad functional categories are the key to the main structure of the book. Because the detailed, day-to-day, operational arrangements of housing finance vary according to tenure, the main descriptive chapters variously focus on the owner occupied, independent rented and local authority rented tenure sectors. In addition, in order to maintain the coherence of the underlying organising frame, chapters 3, 4 and 5 concentrate on the financial arrangements associated with the provision of housing and chapters 6, 7 and 8 concentrate on the financial arrangements associated with the management of housing.

The book's overall structure thus allows for two modes of use. By reading the chapters sequentially, the reader will gain an overview of the subject which allows the detailed, descriptive information to be seen in a broad context and to be understood in terms of a model of functional analysis. By reading selected chapters, the reader is able to acquire specific operational information as it relates to particular tenure arrangements.

David Garnett
Barbara Reid
Helen Riley

Bristol
November 1989

Part 1
Introduction

Chapter 1
The nature of housing and housing finance

The nature of a house

In using the term 'house' we mean it to apply to any building or part of a building used as a unit of residential accommodation. Housing possesses a number of features which together set it apart from other commodities. A house has a potential to provide shelter and personal space for a succession of occupiers. In addition it can be a secure investment for its owner providing rental income, capital appreciation or both. In other words, a house can be regarded as being at one and the same time a consumer good, an investment good and a social good. An ability to recognise the simultaneous existence of these categories in relation to a house provides a sound and sensible starting point for anyone wishing to understand what housing finance is about.

Housing as an item of consumption
A house is a consumer item in that it generates utility in the form of a stream of housing services which individuals and families need or want. In other words, the primary reason that most people seek access to housing is to consume and enjoy all the various things it provides that together go to constitute a 'home'. These include *shelter* in the form of physical security, *location* in the form of convenient proximity to work, shops, schools, countryside, etc., and, less tangibly, benefits such as *status* which may relate to the size or design of the house.

It is sometimes said that housing, like food and clothing, is a primary consumer good because without it a reasonably decent life is not possible. In other words, it is argued that housing is no ordinary consumer item, but a 'consumer necessity'. This argument is, however, limited as the quantity and quality of the housing enjoyed by many better-off families is more than that needed to satisfy what society currently regards as its minimum housing standards. Over the last one hundred years or so society has used central and local government machinery to establish and enforce minimum housing standards and it is the wish to maintain such standards that is often pointed to as an underlying explanation of why it is that housing is subsidised.

Another reason given for subsidising the consumption of housing is that it is expensive relative to disposable income. The price of a house is almost invariably equivalent to a multiple of the purchaser's annual income, and for those who rent, the rental charge is likely to represent a high proportion of their outgoings relative to other items in their household budget.

Recognition of the fact that some minimum standard of housing is necessary for all families, and that it is expensive relative to income has had a profound effect on the way in which the system of housing finance has evolved. When households with a preference for ownership are unable to purchase outright they must either rent their homes from landlords or borrow the money to purchase. So two consequences resulting from the nature of housing as a consumer commodity have been the establishment of a rented sector, and the development alongside the market for owner-occupied housing of a parallel money market providing long-term loans to purchasers in the form of mortgages. At different times the State has intervened in different ways to encourage housing consumption by reducing both the price of renting and the price of borrowing.

Housing as investment

Housing can be regarded as an item of personal investment in so far as it is a durable asset with a potential to earn a yield in the form of a rental income or a capital gain. The relative value of the investment is determined by its type, size, quality and geographical location.

Because houses are geographically fixed, a shortage of housing in one area cannot be eased by the existence of a surplus of housing in some other area. A consequence of this is that in those parts of the country which are experiencing above average economic growth, housing investment yields may be rising rapidly while in those areas which are experiencing economic decline, house prices and rents may be rising less rapidly, not at all, or falling.

The existence of this investment potential affects peoples' attitudes towards spending money on the acquisition, improvement or maintenance of houses in which they have proprietary interests. If a house is regarded as an item of consumption the owner or occupier will weigh up the price of buying, renting, repairing or maintaining and compare it with the utility he or she would expect to acquire in return for such an outlay. If, however, a house is regarded by an owner as an investment asset then he or she will weigh up any proposed expenditure and compare it with the anticipated yield resulting from the outlay. Clearly tenants will have a predominantly consumption interest in a house and will tend to be motivated to spend money on it with a view to gaining or maintaining its utility, while a landlord will have a predominantly investment interest and will be largely motivated to spend money on a house with a view to maximising its yield. An owner-occupier, however, has both a consumption and an investment interest in a property and will tend to bear both of these characteristics in mind when purchasing, improving or maintaining it.

Housing as a social asset
To the extent that its provision and maintenance is seen to be of concern to the wider community, housing possesses characteristics which can lead to it being classified as a social commodity.

Because nearly all houses are built to a standard which ensures that they outlive their initial owners and occupiers, housing production caters for future as well as for current housing needs and demands. In this sense housing can be regarded as a national social asset, held in trust by one generation for the next. Furthermore, there is a recognised, albeit ill-defined, link between housing conditions and health, crime and educational performance. Also, the condition of an individual housing unit has a 'spill-over effect' on the use values and exchange values of neighbouring properties. For all these reasons it is possible to argue that there exists a community interest in housing which is over and above the proprietary interests of owners and occupiers.

The existence of a non-proprietary, community interest in the size and quality of the housing stock is pointed to as another reason for directing public expenditure into the housing system.

The nature of housing finance

Housing finance is concerned with the system of money and credit which operates to enable all types of residential property to be built, improved, bought, rented, maintained and repaired.

Because the operational practices and procedures associated with the financing of owner occupied housing and the various forms of private and public rented housing all differ somewhat, much of the later descriptive content of this book is organised around a tenure framework. It is, however, essential to begin by recognising the fact that the underlying principles of housing finance are independent of tenure. This chapter considers a number of ways of categorising housing finance which are not tenure specific. These ways of thinking about housing finance need to be grasped at the outset because they determine the way in which the rest of the book is structured and they permeate the tenure analysis which follows in later chapters.

One way of appreciating the nature and scope of housing finance is to analyse the purposes to which financial resources are put (see Figure 1.1.1). This approach of focusing attention on the housing functions which have to be financed is useful on two counts. Firstly, it provides a

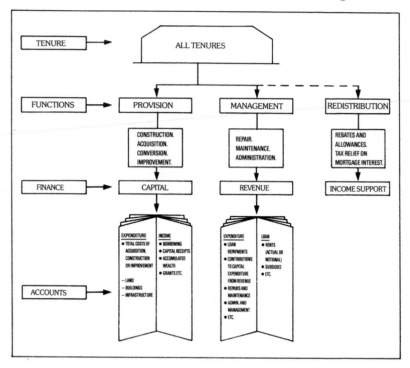

Figure 1.1.1 The system of housing finance

coherent and easily understood conceptual framework for our analysis. Secondly, it acts as a reminder that the raising and spending of money is not an end in itself, and that financial policies and practices should be judged by their effectiveness in helping to achieve society's practical housing objectives.

Before itemising the specific and detailed housing functions that have to be financed, we need to identify some broad financial categories. In particular, it will be useful to distinguish between finance that is used for *capital purposes,* finance that is used for *revenue purposes* and finance that is used for *income support purposes.*

Capital expenditure is that incurred for the purpose of acquiring fixed capital formation. Fixed capital formation is composed of assets of a relatively permanent nature, and in a housing context may be thought of as anything which increases the supply or quality of the housing stock. It includes the fees of lawyers, architects and other professionals in connection with the purchase of land and existing buildings as well as all the material, labour and other costs incurred in connection with the erection of new dwellings. Money spent on converting or improving (as against maintaining and repairing) the existing stock of dwellings results in more or better quality housing being available, and for this reason should be regarded as capital expenditure in the same way as money spent on the building of completely new units is regarded as capital expenditure.

Capital income Capital expenditure is typically financed out of accumulated savings or borrowing, but can be financed by revenue contributions or gifts. In the context of housing, capital expenditure is largely financed by borrowing. In practice the term 'capital income' is seldom used. Income of this nature is generally referred to as 'capital receipts' and includes money received from the sale of capital assets such as dwellings sold by local authorities under the 'Right to Buy' provisions of recent legislation.

Revenue expenditure is that incurred in acquiring consumable and other non-permanent goods and services. Revenue expenditure is often referred to as 'current' or 'consumption' expenditure and sometimes as 'costs in use'. In a housing context it may be thought of as those recurring payments on general administration, loan interest and debt redemption together with those payments made for the purpose of maintaining, repairing and managing the housing stock. In other words, revenue expenditure is all expenditure incurred in the day-to-day provision of housing services together with that incurred for the purpose of maintaining the capital assets in a state of working efficiency. Because the costs of servicing loans taken out to purchase capital items are regarded as part of revenue expenditure, capital expenditure decisions can have significant revenue implications. Revenue expenditure is met from revenue income.

Revenue income is derived from employment or trading earnings, subsidies or from the ownership of assets. In a housing context, revenue income is that income derived from the ownership of housing. In the case of private landlords the recurring revenue costs associated with their properties are normally met out of the rents they receive from their tenants. Housing associations meet such costs out of rents received and subsidies from the Housing Corporation. Local authority housing revenue income may comprise rents received from tenants, government subsidies, interest arising from the sale of council houses financed by council mortgages and rate fund contributions. At first sight it would appear that owner occupiers derive no revenue income from their houses. However, it can be argued that the revenue income of owner occupiers exists in the form of the notional rents they would have to pay were they renting their properties.

The relationship between capital and revenue expenditure.
The difference between capital and revenue is a theoretical one, and in practice, accounting procedures and conventions sometimes blur this distinction. What gets counted as capital or revenue may, for example, be determined by what funds are available. This has to be kept in mind when considering how various institutions actually classify their expenditure: for example, capital works may be financed from revenue. It is also important to reiterate the point made above that capital expenditure decisions will often carry with them implications for future revenue expenditure.

Income support. We have stressed the point that for most people, housing is expensive relative to disposable income. This fact, coupled with society's desire to make it possible for all families to be adequately housed to some acceptable standard, has led governments at different times to introduce various subsidy arrangements alongside the system of housing finance. Since 1981 the term 'housing benefit' has come to be associated specifically with the unified system of rebates and payments which was introduced in that year. As explained in chapter 8, this system is administered through local authority housing departments. Despite that, housing benefit remains an integral part of the Government's Social Security budget and as such is not, strictly speaking, part of the system of housing finance but rather part of the system of welfare finance.

In the context of the present discussion the notion of *income support* covers more than the system of housing benefit. In other words, 'income support' is here taken to refer to all forms of subsidy or financial help which is designeeed to make the consumption of housing or housing related services cheaper in real terms. In this sense, for example, owner occupiers who enjoy tax relief on their mortgage interest payments can be said to be receiving financial 'benefit'.

Housing functions and housing finance

Having broadly categorised housing finance in terms of capital, revenue and income support we are in a position to itemise the various purposes to which money and credit is put.

Provision
The function of *capital finance* is to pay for new dwellings and for the acquisition and improvement of existing ones: it is needed to build and to buy. It is used to pay for 'provision' in the widest sense of the word. The real capital formation it provides may be privately owned as in the case of owner occupied or privately rented houses, or publicly owned as in the case of council houses. Because council houses are provided and owned by a public authority, they are sometimes referred to as 'social capital'. It should be recognised that a private housing development will involve the spending of public money capital on the provision of items of real social capital such as roads, sewers, schools, etc.

Houses may contain certain items of relatively immobile equipment such as central heating and double glazing which are generally regarded as integral parts of the building. In new dwellings they are treated as capital formation. In practice, when such items are installed in existing dwellings, they are often paid for out of revenue income. Despite this, because they clearly add to, rather than simply maintain the quality of the property, they are, in principle, provision items. In other words, accounting practice does not always mirror the economists' theoretical distinction between capital and revenue used in this chapter.

Within the provision function 'acquisition' relates to the finance which is used to buy houses which already exist. Owner occupiers and private landlords are the main purchasers of second-hand houses, although all local authorities and most housing associations do acquire properties which they usually improve or convert before letting to tenants. Private developers sometimes acquire blocks of dwellings or individual units which they convert or improve and then sell on to private buyers.

Much 'conversion' activity takes the form of altering large dwelling units into a greater number of smaller units.

Management
Once the real fixed capital formation has been built or acquired, capital expenditure ceases (with the exception of any later improvements), and the owner and/or occupier is then faced with all the recurring 'costs in use' which we have classified above as revenue expenditure. These costs stem from the need to manage the assets on a day-to-day basis.

Within the management function 'administration' refers to monies used to deliver the range of supervisory and support services landlords provide for their tenants and others. In a housing association or local authority housing department this will include a central administration charge and will also allow for the employment of specialist staff. Some of these employees will operate at a professional level as housing officers and be responsible for administering the procedures associated with allocations, rent collection, the management of maintenance and providing aid and advice to committees, tenants and the general public. Others will be employed at a more operational level to provide such facilities as cleaning, warden support for the elderly, caretaking, and so on.

All houses have to be managed irrespective of the tenure arrangements. In this sense, private landlords and owner occupiers are just as much housing managers as are the employees of housing associations and local authority housing departments. Some day-to-day housing management functions, such as decorating or minor repairs, may be carried out by tenants. Indeed, some of the managerial responsibilities of tenants may be specified in a lease or tenancy agreement.

Redistribution
Along with the housing finance system, the social security system operates to redistribute real incomes. Broadly speaking, this works by the central government collecting taxation, part of which it then redistributes in the form of housing and social security benefits. Owner occupiers receive taxation concessions rather than direct payments or reduced charges.

Redistribution in the form of subsidies, payments, rebates and allowances occurs for two broad reasons. It may occur in order to help low income families meet their housing expenses. The subsidisation of housing expenses can take many forms and as we will see in the next chapter, the current trend is towards more reliance on fiscal welfare measures (income support) and less emphasis on supply-side ('bricks and mortar') subsidies. Alternatively, it may occur because the government of the day wishes to encourage the consumption of a particular type of housing. The Conservative administrations of the 1980s, for example, have wanted to encourage owner occupation, and have accordingly maintained the system of mortgage tax relief.

Accounting and audit

The records of expenditure and income for a given period are kept in accounts. The production of audited accounts is an important aspect of the procedure by which those who manage an organisation are made accountable for their actions to some authority such as a body of shareholders, a management committee, councillors or ratepayers.

Types and styles of accounts
Most organisations produce annual accounts and some are legally required to do so. During the year the organisation will record all of its financial transactions and at the end of the year these records will be used to produce the final accounts.

The final accounts consist of an account which shows the income and expenditure for the year and a balance sheet which lists the assets and liabilities held by the organisation at the end of the year. The assets held will include such things as buildings and land, stocks of goods and debts owed to the organisation. The liabilities include the amounts owed by the organisation to others in respect of capital (loans, etc.) and revenue (sundry creditors) commitments.

Although all organisations produce accounts and balance sheets, this does not mean that these all look alike or contain the same sort of information: the style of the accounts used will be determined by the needs of the organisation. For instance, the accounts of a company contain details of its trading activities, profits made and distributions to shareholders. The accounts of a local authority detail expenditure and income on the various services that it has the duty or power to provide together with local tax receipts and Exchequer subsidies. Owner occupiers are not required to keep accounts as they are not responsible to others for their housing decisions, but they may choose to keep records for their own information.

The nature and interpretation of accounts
While accountancy and account keeping demand professional skills and qualifications, accounts can generally be considered simply as the *recording in financial terms* of the activities undertaken by the organisation in question. From properly prepared annual accounts it should be possible, even for the completely uninitiated, to comprehend the nature of an organisation's transactions during the period covered.

Accounts are prepared according to the *prudence principle*. This means that, as far as possible, accountants work with facts rather than opinion and with past events rather than with future ones. Most accounts are prepared on the *historic* basis and use market-related values. Because accounts do not deal with the future directly, those wishing to use accounts for planning purposes will need to identify trends from past transactions.

Most people who use accounts are not so much interested in being able to do the bookkeeping involved in their preparation, as being able to understand and interpret the information recorded in them. As well as allowing for the appraisal of past results, accounts are a source of financial and statistical information which can be used to provide guidance for future policy. By careful analysis of accounting records it may be possible to bring to light data which will assist in identifying waste and inappropriate management decisions and help to suggest reforms and economies. In order to use and make sense of accounts it is important to have an appreciation of what the end result is intended to achieve.

Can accounts measure success?
If the organisation's aims can be expressed simply in terms of money, then accounts can be designed to show whether these aims are being achieved. For example, they can be used to show whether the rent charged by a landlord is sufficient to cover the costs of providing the accommodation and earn profit. However, current accounting practice cannot give clear guidance in relation to an organisation's more complex concerns, such as whether the rate of juvenile crime will be reduced as a result of the refurbishment of a run down estate or whether homeless families will be better off in a hostel or in bed-and-breakfast accommodation.

Accountants rarely introduce evaluative goals into published accounts, even when quantification of such goals would not be controversial. It is for the user of accounts to determine criteria for measuring an organisation's success and to find evidence of achievement from a wide range of sources of which the published accounts will be just one.

External audit
Once accounts have been prepared they must be audited. This means that accountants specialising in audit work check the accounts and certify that they have been prepared in accordance with legislation and good accounting practice. The auditors must be independent of the organisation whose accounts are being checked and they cannot be employees of that organisation.

Internal audit
Large organisation also have internal auditors who will be employees and whose job it is to ensure that the financial systems of the organisation are properly designed and implemented. Such internal auditors should be as independent as possible.

Summary

This chapter has looked at the characteristics of housing as a commodity and considered the nature and scope of housing finance in very general terms. Its intention has been to provide a simple conceptual framework within which to locate the more detailed analysis that follows. The introduction to accounting and auditing sketched the framework of financial reporting as it applies to organisations of all kinds. The accounting and audit practices of the organisations that provide housing services will be considered in detail in later chapters. The actual system of housing finance has evolved over a long period and with this evolution has come a wide range of financial practices and procedures which give the appearance of great complexity. The best way of dealing with this apparent confusion is to hold to a model of the overall system which is clear and coherent. In this way, and only in this way, will it be appreciated that in essence, housing finance is a quite straightforward subject.

The model we have built here is based on a consideration of the broad uses to which financial resources are put. In subsequent chapters this approach is developed largely in terms of a tenure analysis. The next chapter will consider the position of the state in relation to public expenditure and housing finance and the following three chapters are concerned with the part finance plays in the 'provision' of housing. Chapters 6 to 8 consider the financial aspects of the 'management' of housing.

Chapter 2
The State and housing finance

In Chapter 1 we stressed the point that housing is a commodity which is of particular importance to the social and economic well-being of both individuals and the wider community. It is recognition of this importance that lies behind much of the State's involvement over the years in the housing system and its associated financial arrangements.

Before considering how the system of housing finance relates to wider social and economic policy concerns we need to make the point that all policy formation and enactment operates within, and is affected by, political aims and objectives. In this way it can be argued that housing finance policy is affected by broader social and economic policy considerations which in turn are largely derived from political values and attitudes.

Political context

Government actions have to take account of social and economic factors which are not directly under its control or influence. For example, policies relating to housing, health, education and so on will, to some extent, be affected by such things as the changing structure of the population, divorce rates, world commodity prices and peoples' expectations of the Welfare State. However, despite this, a good deal of what governments say and do is planned rather than reactive: that is, it relates directly to their political aims and manifesto pledges. In short, it is affected by their policy positions.

It should be recognised that policies are not arbitrarily plucked out of the air but are derived from the values and attitudes of the policy-makers. In the recent history of housing it is possible to detect two broadly distinct and competing approaches underlying the various policy changes which have occurred throughout the period. Simply put, some policy enactments have been derived from what might be termed a *market ideology* and others from what might be termed a *welfare ideology*.

Two broad agendas
Although it is beyond the scope of this book to describe the detailed history of housing policy, it is useful for the student of housing finance to be aware that, broadly speaking, legislative changes have been driven by two competing political views about society's economic objectives. *Market ideology* is grounded in the belief that free enterprise tends to be naturally efficient and fair, and that the activities associated with the provision, consumption and exchange of housing should, as far as possible, be conducted by private individuals or firms rather than by the agents of central or local government. It tends to favour rent policies related to market prices and replacement costs rather than to people's ability to pay or to historic costs. It also tends to advocate subsidy arrangements which put purchasing power into peoples' pockets rather than those which are designed to lower or suppress market prices. That is, it tends to favour welfare arrangements which increase the incomes of poor families so as to give them more effective market power, rather than promoting policies which subsidise production or impose price controls. This is because both production subsidies and price controls are seen as distorting the market by keeping prices 'artificially' low by inhibiting or preventing them from rising to their market levels. Because it embraces the notion of 'self-reliance', market ideology is sympathetic to the idea that owner occupation is the 'natural' and 'normal' tenure arrangement for most people.
Welfare ideology is grounded in the belief that certain commodities have a social importance which is so great that the State should guarantee some minimum standard of provision for everyone. It emphasises the notion of *need* rather than the notion of *demand,* and it represents the value system which underlies what is popularly referred to as 'the Welfare State'. It has been instrumental in developing the concept of *welfare rights,* and in the housing field is associated with the proposition that *every* household should have a decent home at a price they can afford. It tends to be sympathetic both to price control (or regulation) arrangements and to the provision of production subsidies where these are designed to reduce the price of housing for low income families. In general it sees an active role for central and local government in the housing system.
    The following schema, Figure 1.2.1. illustrates how the two ideologies lead to different housing finance practices depending on the policy adopted. As a generalisation, market ideology tends to lead to income support measures while welfare ideology tends to be more sympathetic to the provision of 'bricks-and-mortar' subsidies.

MARKET		WELFARE

<table>
<tr><td>Ideology</td><td rowspan="7" align="center">T
H
E
O
R
Y</td><td>Ideology</td></tr>
<tr><td>Notion of 'self-reliance' within an enterprise culture</td><td>Notions of 'entitlement' and 'welfare rights'</td></tr>
<tr><td>Policy</td><td>Policy</td></tr>
<tr><td>Emphasis on 'effective demand' and market mechanisms</td><td>Emphasis on 'social need' and Welfare State</td></tr>
</table>

Delivery		Delivery
Market-related rents (e.g. 'fair rents')	P R A C T I C E	Rents related to historic costs and ability to pay (e.g. 'reasonable rents')
Income support in the form of tax relief, rebates, allowances, etc.		Production subsidies (e.g. Exchequer grants to local authorities and HAG)
Measures to encourage owner occupation		Measures to support public provision of housing

Figure 1.2.1

Although market ideology is generally associated with the political 'right' and welfare ideology with the political 'left', it would be an over-simplification to say that these two world views exactly mirror the party political divide in Britain over this century. For example, the Conservative administrations of the 1950s directed large-scale financial support in the form of production grants towards the provision of council housing while at the same time pursuing a market ideology by relaxing controls on private sector rents. In recent years, despite its general commitment to welfare ideology, the Labour Party has, for politically pragmatic reasons, supported measures designed to increase access to owner occupation. For such reasons it is more useful to think of two *ideological* rather than two strictly *party political* agendas competing for prominence in the housing policies of recent time.

Social context

The emergence of social concern
Nineteenth century *laissez faire* market attitudes remained largely unchallenged until a coherent and systematic welfare agenda began to emerge in the last quarter of the century. By this time there was much official and journalistic comment linking overcrowded and squalid living conditions with such social and moral evils as incest, prostitution and petty crime. But government intervention was most of all stimulated

by the growing contemporary awareness of the relationship between insanitary housing and the incidence of communicable diseases such as cholera and typhoid. Once the State began to intervene to establish minimum standards of housing provision as part of its drive to improve public health, the question of housing subsidies became an issue. The law prevented free market forces from adjusting housing standards downwards in line with the limited incomes of working class people. As a result a more obvious gap emerged between the rent paying capacity of many households and the rent levels that needed to be charged by the market to provide less over-crowded and better quality dwellings. Simply put, once the State had intervened to improve housing standards, it brought to the fore the question of how the improved conditions should be paid for. It became clear that to realise fully the original health and housing policy objectives, additional interventionist measures were required.

After 1914 three broad strategies were adopted: rent control and regulation, the public provision of subsidised houses for the 'working classes' and the encouragement of area-based slum-clearance schemes. In addition, later in the century, financial assistance was also directed to the housing association movement and tax concessions and income support measures were introduced to help people meet their housing-related expenses.

The qualified achievements of intervention
In this way it can be argued that the social rationale for intervention relates to society's desire to increase both the quantity and quality of the nation's housing stock and to help low income families to gain access to decent homes which are appropriate to their needs. In many respects the interventionist measures have been successful, and some recent commentators have argued that a prominent feature of Britain's recent housing history has been the closing of the post-Second World War gap which existed between the number of households and the number of dwellings. Between 1951 and 1980 the rate of growth of housing units was faster than the rate of growth of households, thereby creating an officially recorded crude national surplus of stock. Figures based on census and other official data indicate that a deficit of some 800,000 dwellings in 1951 had been transformed into an apparent surplus of 200,000 by 1971, and that this small crude surplus had increased to about one million by 1980. The figures suggest that since 1980 the rates of growth of the housing stock and of households have remained more or less equal.

Although this officially recognised surplus has allowed some commentators to argue that, in general terms, housing need in Britain has been satisfied, such a crude comparison between the size of the total stock and the total number of households does not by itself show whether there are sufficient dwellings, and it certainly tells us nothing about the adequacy of the stock in terms of quality. As we will see in later chapters, there is currently a great deal of concern that the stock is deteriorating at a faster rate than it is being improved.

Apart from crucial questions about the fitness of the stock, the 'surplus' masks the existence of severe local and regional shortages and takes no account of the hundreds of thousands of 'concealed households' made up of young adults, couples and one-parent families who live as part of someone else's (often a parent's) household. It does not tell us anything about the relationship between housing costs and the ability to meet them, nor does it take account of the fact that not all of the dwellings are available for occupation (e.g. second homes, temporary voids and unlet properties held vacant with a view to sale). All of these qualifications mean that housing problems persist and that many households are still in housing need.

Despite these important qualifications, the global figures do indicate that, as an historical trend, over the last one hundred years, general housing conditions for the mass of the British people have greatly improved. Much of this achievement has been the result of the financial provisions associated with the various forms of government intervention into the housing system.

These provisions constitute an important part of the mechanism by which money and credit pass through the housing system so as to enable all types of residential property to be built, improved, bought, rented, maintained and repaired. The arrangements operate within a legal and administrative framework established by Acts of Parliament and ministerial directives, and since the end of the First World War this framework has been subjected to a continuous stream of reforms and modifications which have stemmed from changes and shifts in government policy. Furthermore, the effectiveness of the framework has been crucially dependent upon funding from the public purse. It is not just a question of the level of public expenditure being directed into the housing system, but also a matter of which individuals and organisations are in receipt of the funding and the conditions which are attached to their application.

Public expenditure policy is largely determined by the Government's approach to managing the economy. The distribution and control of public expenditure is determined by the operational relationships that exist between central government and the various spending organisations and institutions. The key relationship has been that between central and local government.

Economic context

Controlling public expenditure

In recent years controlling the growth of public expenditure has been an important aspect of economic policy. This relates partly to the assumption that there is a link between high levels of public expenditure and inflation, and partly to the current Conservative Government's political commitment to cultivate the market economy and to 'roll back the frontiers of the State'. It favours an argument derived from monetarist economic theory which suggests that high levels of public expenditure create inflationary pressures. Simply put, the argument runs as follows. Public expenditure has to be paid for either by public sector borrowing or out of taxation. Increased borrowing involves an expansion of credit and thereby effectively, an increase in the money supply. If the increased credit base is not matched by an equivalent increase in national output, additional money demand will be chasing (approximately) the same volume of output, and prices will be bid up as a result. If, however, the public expenditure is paid for by raising taxes, any increases in indirect taxation may be passed on directly in the form of higher prices. On the other hand, increases in income taxation may lead to price increases if higher production costs result from compensatory wage claims.

Before considering what is involved in public expenditure planning and management, we need to consider more precisely what is meant by the term 'public expenditure' and we will also need to consider what is meant by 'housing expenditure' in this context.

What is public expenditure?

There is no single definitive meaning of the term 'public expenditure': the definition used largely depends upon the purpose in hand.

Current official definition   Public expenditure is defined for purposes of central planning and management as that expenditure of central government, local authorities and public corporations which has to be financed by borrowing, taxation or national insurance contributions. This official Treasury definition of what constitutes public spending is the one used by the Public Expenditure Survey Committee (PESC) and is described and analysed in the annual White Paper on the Government's Expenditure Plans (see below).

The planning total relates to the public sector as a whole and is defined primarily for use as a control total. The White Paper statistics make a distinction between this *planning total* and *general government expenditure* which relates only to expenditure of central and local government.

The bulk of central government expenditure is financed by money voted by Parliament in the *Supply Estimates*. The biggest exclusion from the Supply Estimates is expenditure from the National Insurance Fund which accounts for most of spending in social security.

Changes with effect from 1989

In a White Paper published in July 1988 *A New Public Expenditure Planning Total* (Cm.441), the Government proposed a change in the coverage of the planning total, to take into account the new arrangements for local government finance due to come into effect in England and Wales in 1990. The 1989 public expenditure survey was the first conducted on the new basis.

Under these new arrangements the Government's public expenditure planning total includes: spending on its own programmes, grants paid to local authorities, the credit approvals it issues for local authority borrowing for capital expenditure, the payments to local authorities from the proceeds of the national non-domestic rate, the external financing limits of public corporations, and a reserve. The idea of the proposal is that the new planning total will include those elements for which central government is responsible and exclude spending which local authorities determine and finance for themselves. Unlike the community charge, non-domestic rates will be set nationally rather than by individual local authorities and will thus be included.

The format of the 1989 White Paper was changed as a preliminary step in the process of transferring the responsibility for departmental chapters from the Treasury to the individual departments. This changed format involved producing the departmental chapters as separate booklets which could be purchased separately (prior to 1989 they appeared in one volume). When responsibility is formally transferred to the departments (probably 1991) there will also be a change in the timing of the publication so that the departmental reports will be published in March at about the same time as the Supply Estimates. Much of the general information relating to public expenditure planning is now included in a supplement to the Autumn Statement (see below) with the remainder being included in a supplementary booklet published with the departmental analyses which constitute the White Paper.

The public sector borrowing requirement (PSBR)   For the purposes of public expenditure planning and management, the public sector is deemed to comprise central government, local authorities and public corporations.[1] The difference between what the public sector collects in taxes and charges and what it spends is known as the *public sector borrowing requirement.* In other words, the PSBR is a financial indicator which measures the extent to which the public sector borrows from other sectors of the economy and from overseas to finance the gap between its expenditures and receipts.

Broader Definitions   It is important to recognise that the official definition is based on administrative convenience rather than economic rationality: there are other ways in which public expenditure might sensibly be defined. In particular, economists sometimes argue that the official definition is too narrow because it concentrates only on monies spent and does not include revenue foregone through discounts or revenue not collected because of tax concessions.

Defining housing expenditure

The official net expenditure on housing as defined in the Expenditure White Paper, covers current spending on subsidies and administration, plus capital expenditure on new public sector building, refurbishment of public sector stock, support for owner occupiers through low-cost home ownership initiatives and improvement grants, minus receipts (mainly from the sale of public sector dwellings).

In 1987-88 the spending organisations to whom the funds were made available were local authorities (about 76 per cent), the Housing Corporation (about 23 per cent), and New Towns (about 1 per cent). From

1988-89 onwards the Government's public expenditure plans provide an allocation for the development of Housing Action Trusts which will be responsible for the renovation of run-down estates formerly in local authority ownership.

For expenditure planning purposes, the Housing Corporation, New Towns and Housing Action Trusts are categorised as *public corporations,* and as such should be distinguished from local authorities.

There are two significant categories of public expenditure on housing which do not appear in the White Paper's housing programme.

1. Housing benefit appears in the Social Security programme. Social Security is the largest single programme category, accounting for about a third of the total. In this programme, 55 per cent is for expenditure on contributory benefits financed from the National Insurance Fund.
2. The following relief to owner occupiers is not officially defined as public spending at all:
   (a) foregone tax on mortgage interest payments[2];
   (b) exemptions from capital gains tax on the sale of a family's main residence;
   (c) discounts on the sale of public sector dwellings.

How is public expenditure measured?
Planning totals are officially measured in cash terms and are generally presented in the White Paper as 'outturn' or 'estimated outturn' figures. In March 1981 the then Chancellor of the Exchequer stated that in the annual reviews of expenditure, spending Departments would, from the start of the process, conduct their discussions and negotiations in terms of the *cash* that would be available. 'Outturn' and 'estimated outturn' describe expenditure actually incurred or estimates made on the basis of partial information.

It is important to recognise that cash measures do not take account of inflation and this makes it difficult to get an accurate picture of the real (volume) changes that occur from year to year. In an attempt to estimate volume changes, the figures are sometimes presented as a proportion of Gross Domestic Product (National Output). However, Gross Domestic Product itself changes over time, and the only real measure of volume changes is one that relates to a base year and constant survey prices.

Ways of categorising public expenditure
There are all sorts of ways in which public expenditure might be classified. For our purposes we need to consider the following categories: spending authority; function or programme; capital and revenue; economic significance.

Public expenditure by spending authority.   The White Paper identifies three broad spending authorities: central government, local authorities and public corporations. Central government is by far the largest spender, followed by local authorities. For example, the 1988 White Paper showed a planning total for 1988-89 of £156.8 bn[3]. Of this total, £114.2 bn or 73 per cent was planned for central government spending, £42.6 bn or

27 per cent was planned for local authorities and £1.4 bn or 0.9 per cent was planned for public corporations. In addition to these planned expenditures, a reserve of £3.5 bn was planned for and an inflow of some £5 bn was anticipated from privatisation proceeds.

Public expenditure by function The main programme areas identified in the White Paper are shown in Table 1.2.1.

As well as the spending programme categories, the White Paper identifies totals for 'Reserves' and 'Privatisation Proceeds'. The Reserve is intended to cover all contingencies including any unexpected national crises, unexpected changes in demand-led programmes (e.g. a rise in unemployment) as well as any expenses related to policy changes and new initiatives occurring in the course of the planning year. Figures for asset sales are included in the main programme totals, but they are *deducted* from the total because they represent an *inflow* rather than an outflow of monies.

General Government Debt Interest is not included as part of the overall planning total, but is added to that total along with other national accounts adjustments to get the figure for General Government Expenditure (see above for definition). This is because it is not possible to associate debt interest with any particular programme.

Capital and current expenditure [4] The broad definition of *capital spending* used in the White Paper covers payments by the public sector to either renew or increase the nation's stock of physical assets. It covers expenditure on fixed assets (net of certain asset sales), stockbuilding, capital grants and net lending to the private sector. The wages and salaries of certain people engaged in planning and supervising capital projects are included, and for local authorities, it also includes the capital value of assets acquired under financial leases, property leased for more than 20 years, and all vehicles leased for more than one year.

The broad definition of *current spending* used in the White Paper covers payments made by the public sector on providing services, and largely consists of the wages and salaries of central and local government employees and the purchase of consumable goods and services by public

Table 1.2.1 Percentage shares of public expenditure

Year	1978–79	1986–87	1990–91
Social security	25.8	31.9	32.4
Education & science	14.4	13.3	13.7
Health	11.9	13.1	14.1
Defence	11.4	12.6	12.6
Law & order	3.7	4.8	5.3
Housing	8.0	4.1	3.8
Transport	4.9	4.0	3.7
Industry, trade & energy	5.1	2.4	1.0
Agriculture, fisheries & food	1.6	1.6	1.7

Source: based on 1988 White Paper Vol. 1. Chart 1.10.

sector organisations. It includes local authority payments of such things as mandatory student awards and rent rebates and allowances as part of Housing Benefit. Both local authority and central government spending is measured net of VAT.

The distinction between capital and current expenditure is of some economic significance, in that capital investment in industry and the social fabric is seen as an essential element in the maintenance of long term economic prosperity and social well-being, while much current expenditure is directly channelled into employment. Another way in which public expenditure can be categorised is in terms of its economic significance.

Public expenditure by economic significance   The aggregate figure for public expenditure falls into two distinct economic categories:

  (a) expenditure on goods and services, and,

  (b) expenditure on transfer payments and loans.

Expenditure on goods and services consists of current expenditure by central government and local authorities and expenditure on fixed assets by central government, local authorities and public corporations. Such expenditure represents a real use of resources by the public sector: it absorbs physical resources from the economy which are then used up in the production of housing, health, defence, education, and transport services, etc. In other words, they represent a measure of the State's economic activity.

Transfer payments include such items as student grants, Housing Benefit, subsidies to the private sector, state pensions and other social security payments. They involve a redistribution of money wealth from one set of private hands to another set of private hands and, as such, they are not directly used to finance public sector economic activity (see Figure 1.2.2). If we make the assumption that those who pay the most taxes do not receive the most transfer payments, then we can say that such payments *redistribute* rather than *absorb* resources.

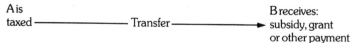

A is
taxed ———————— Transfer ————————→ B receives:
subsidy, grant
or other payment

Figure 1.2.2

Transfer payments have a direct *social welfare* effect but only an indirect *economic* effect. The indirect economic effect results from the fact that the less well off receivers of transfers will have a tendency to spend a higher proportion of their income than the better off givers. This means that the transfers will affect the nature and scope of consumer spending and savings in the economy.

This way of categorising public expenditure allows for a more penetrating analysis of the global figures. It underlines the point that figures which show the growth in total expenditure may be masking a number of interesting social, economic and political issues. For example, it is often argued that increases in public expenditure result in a redistribution of resources away from the private and towards the public sector of the economy. This is clearly not necessarily true. Transfer payments, which in recent years have been the fastest growing element of public expenditure, may 'simply' have the effect of redistributing resources between individuals and firms operating within the private sector.

Resource expenditure, transfer payments and housing
As we have seen, resource expenditure relates to money committed to the direct production of economic goods and services. In a housing context resource expenditure can be in a *capital* form as in the case of money spent on increasing the quantity or quality of the stock (including loans to the private sector for this purpose), or in a *current* form as in the case of money spent on managing the stock and providing housing aid and advice services.

Transfer expenditure related to housing involves the making of payments in the form of grants and subsidies which are transferred from the accounts of local or central government to other institutions, organisations and individuals. Unlike resource expenditure, such payments are not made in return for a contribution to economic activity, but represent a shift in effective demand (spending power) from one group to another and, strictly speaking, are made as a consequence of welfare policy rather than housing policy. Housing Benefit is perhaps the most common form of transfer expenditure dealt with by housing practitioners.

Recent trends in the level of housing expenditure: White Paper programme[5]
In recent years the White Paper programme area 'Housing' (see page 17 for definition) has suffered severe real cuts. In money terms, the figure for 'DoE-Housing' has fallen from £4.5 bn in 1979-80 (outturn) to £2.4 bn in 1987-88 (estimated outturn). In real terms (using 1986-87 as a base year) this represents a reduction of 32 per cent. Table 1.2.1 shows that Housing's share of the total expenditure allocation has fallen from 8 per cent in 1978-79 to 4.1 per cent in 1986-87 and is planned to fall to 3.8 per cent in 1990-91. The Table also gives a clear indication of how badly Housing has fared in comparison with other programmes. The most obvious practical effects of these substantial cuts have been a reduction in public sector house building and a reduction in the frequency of repairs and maintenance of the existing public stock.

Recent trends in housing expenditure: broad definition[6]
The dramatic cutbacks in the housing programme have to be seen against wider changes in public spending on Housing Benefit, mortgage interest tax relief, capital gains concessions and discounts on council and other public sector housing sales, made in the same period.

In 1979-80 there were 1,425,000 recipients claiming £278mn worth of Housing Benefit in the form of rent rebates and allowances. By

1986-87 the number of recipients had risen to 5,010,000 and they were claiming £3,154mn of benefit. In 1985-86 the annual amount distributed in Housing Benefit (just over £3.0bn) was about the same as the figure for the White Paper housing programme. In 1986-87, for the first time, the figure for Housing Benefit (£3.1bn) was significantly higher than that for the White Paper housing programme (£2.6bn).

Similarly, in 1987-88 Exchequer revenue foregone in the form of mortgage interest tax relief, was about twice the sum of the outturn for the White Paper housing programme of that year: the outturn was £2,703mn while the figure for mortgage interest tax relief was around £5bn. These figures represent a significant change in the situation over recent years. In 1979-80, for example, Exchequer income foregone in the form of mortgage interest tax relief was only about a third of the level of the White Paper programme figure for that year.

Allowance should also be made for the fact that Exchequer revenue is foregone as a consequence of capital gains tax not being charged on the rise in values of family homes at a time when house price inflation is often ahead of the rate of general inflation.

Putting all these considerations together, we can argue that, in terms of our broader definition of housing expenditure, financial resources have not been significantly withdrawn from housing, but have rather been redistributed away from local authority provision towards owner occupation and income support.

The planning of public expenditure

Central government's general operational objectives
The Government's 'task' can be thought of as comprising two broad activities:

(a) making a political decision as to what total should be planned for and how that total should be allocated between different programmes; and

(b) controlling and accounting for the actual spending outturns so that the outcomes match the plan and the constitutional requirements of Parliamentary control over the spending of public money are fulfilled.

The PESC planning process and the White Paper
Planning centres around the preparation and publication of the Public Expenditure White Paper. The White Paper can be thought of as the culmination of the process of resource planning and allocation that determines the total level of expenditure and its distribution between the various activities of central and local government.

The Paper is published in the new year before the Budget. Since 1989 it is published as a number of separate booklets or chapters, most of which deal with the expenditure plans of individual departments (see above). One chapter, for example, contains the DoE's plans for housing in England while others cover Scotland, Wales and Northern Ireland. In addition to these chapters, the housing practitioner and student will find much of interest in the chapter covering DSS estimates which includes plans for housing benefit, and the Supplementary Analyses booklet which outlines the overall expenditure plans, categorised in terms similar to those discussed above.

The White Paper covers a specified three year *planning period* and is titled (for example) 'The Government's Expenditure Plans 1989-90 to 1991-92'. It contains firm programme decisions for the financial year ahead and more tentative plans for the remainder of the planning period. Plans for a new terminal year are added each year and the plans for any given year firm up as the year approaches: so, the plans for the year ahead are firm, while those for subsequent years are increasingly provisional.

The general aim is for ministers collectively to review the plans during the summer and autumn and take decisions on them in time for the White Paper to be published in the early part of the calendar year. This review takes place within the framework projected in the Government's *medium term financial strategy* (MTFS) which is published at the start of the financial year alongside the annual Budget. The Budget is the 'symbolic' centre-piece of the Government's planning mechanism. Its traditional function has been to set out how central government intends to raise the revenue to meet expenditure. More recently, it has also been used as an occasion for the Chancellor of the Exchequer to review the progress of economic policies. The MTFS sets out the framework of the Government's economic policy and in recent years has emphasised the Chancellor's intention to bring in measures to limit inflation and encourage economic growth. Since 1979 this has produced a commitment to bring down public spending's share of national income and to reduce the burden of taxation.

The work of public expenditure planning is co-ordinated by the *Public Expenditure Survey Committee* (PESC), an interdepartmental committee of officials chaired by the Treasury and which was set up in 1961 after the Plowden Committee Report.[7] The Committee has given its name to the review process as a whole — often colloquially referred to as the 'PESC planning process'. The Committee's function is to provide the basic facts upon which ministers will take their decisions.

In the late spring, after the Budget, and within the general context of the MTFS, the Treasury begins its discussions with the departments about their spending proposals. At this time each department carries out its own review on a basis which has been approved collectively by ministers earlier in the year. The Treasury issues instructions to each department giving the basic working assumptions upon which plans will be made and the department produces provisional estimates covering a five year period which are sent to the Chief Secretary to the Treasury. The analysis prepared by officials is designed to provide ministers with answers to the following general questions.

1. What is the existing state of the expenditure plans?

Current practice is to define the existing position as the plans in the preceding White Paper, amended to take account of subsequent policy decisions.

2. Where could reductions be made?

This provides ministers with some indication of priorities within their programmes. i.e. The question is asked even when there is no actual intention to cut a particular programme.

The expenditure plans are considered against the forecasts prepared by the Treasury for the growth in the economy over ensuing years, and decisions are made on the basis of such predictions.

In mid summer, once the Chief Secretary has received the provisional estimates, he reports to a special Cabinet meeting at which ministers 'go through the ritual' of pledging their allegiance to an agreed planned expenditure total.

After the summer recess, in September and October, they return to 'squabble' over their share of that total. This takes the form of individual ministers having detailed discussions (referred to as 'bilaterals') with the Chief Secretary which attempt to resolve any conflicts between the departments and the Treasury. If they are unable to agree, the problem is dealt with by a small group of ministers which is chaired by a senior Cabinet minister and is popularly referred to as the 'Star Chamber'. Once the departments and the Treasury are reconciled the Cabinet meet again and by November the final decision on public expenditure is taken.

Once the Cabinet are agreed (usually early November), the Chancellor of the Exchequer publishes his *Autumn Statement* which acts as a trailer for the White Paper expenditure plans to be published in the new year. A supplement to the Autumn Statement is published which includes general information relating to public expenditure and outlines the assumptions behind the planning exercise. This information is later amplified in the White Paper Supplementary Analysis chapter by analysing expenditure in terms of who plans it (department), who spends it (spending authority), where it goes (function and territorial area), and what it is spent on (economic category). This White Paper chapter may also include information on historical trends in public spending and material on matters relating to such things as privatisation proceeds, tax allowances and reliefs, etc.

The control of public expenditure

For their plans to be realised governments need to establish procedures which influence the behaviour of those institutions and organisations that actually do the spending. Historically, local authorities have been used as the primary vehicle for distributing centrally raised public money into the provision of local services including housing. For this reason the operational relationships between central and local government are seen as being of central importance to the effective Treasury control of public expenditure.

Cash limits
Cash limits as a mechanism of control over spending were introduced generally in 1976. Cash limits quite simply set a limit on the amount of cash the Government proposes to spend or authorise on certain services or blocks of services during a particular financial year[8]. Cash limits are published on Budget day with the Supply Estimates.

The majority of cash limits are based on the Supply Estimates (see section on definitions above) and cover direct expenditure by central government and its voted grants and lending to other public sector bodies. About 60 per cent of public expenditure is affected by cash limits. Some 40 per cent of expenditure is directly cash limited and another 20 per cent is indirectly limited in the form of local authority current expenditure. This 20 per cent is controlled because the bulk of the Aggregate Exchequer Grant paid to help local authorities finance their services is subject to cash limits. The nationalised industries' contribution to public expenditure is controlled by means of external financing limits, which are a form of cash limit for individual industries.

Cash limits and local government finance
It is important to note that most of *Aggregate Exchequer Grant* towards local authority current expenditure is subject to cash limits. They also apply to capital expenditure financed by borrowing.

Prior to the Local Government Planning and Land Act 1980, controls on capital expenditure were regulated via a loans sanction procedure which required a local authority to get permission to borrow for specific projects. Controls now apply to expenditure and expenditure programmes as a whole rather than to specific projects. (This is considered more fully in chapter 5.)

Cash limits may have increased awareness of the importance of cash flow management in the public sector and sharpened up attitudes towards cost control. They are also regarded by some as a 'surrogate pay policy' for the public sector because in setting a limit, the Government seems to be taking a view about salaries and wages in the coming year.

Central–local relations

In recent years there has been considerable Government-led questioning of the role of local authorities with respect to the provision of a whole range of local services. One facet of this has resulted in pressure for the privatisation of certain functions such as refuse disposal and office cleaning. Another facet has been the emergence of a view that some areas of service provision would be better handled by non-municipal, single purpose agencies.

In this way we have seen Urban Development Corporations and other specialist agencies being set up to co-ordinate and manage a number of important urban regeneration initiatives. A feature of these organisations is that their boards of management are appointed by the Government and are not elected. In other words they are administrative rather than representative bodies.

In the housing context such bodies have existed since the end of the Second World War in the form of New Towns. The Housing Corporation was set up in 1962 to develop the work of the housing association movement. Housing Action Trusts are the latest version of this kind of corporate involvement in the housing field.

Against the background of these developments the specific relationship between central and local government is changing.

The changing relationship between central and local government
Since 1979, with respect to local government, there has been a shift in emphasis away from *influence and consultation* and towards *control and direction*. This can be seen as part of the Government's desire to limit local government spending as part of its monetary and fiscal strategy for bringing about lower inflation and enhanced international competitiveness while providing for continued growth in output and employment. In short, the need to control local government spending can be seen as an aspect of central Government's attempt to control public expenditure in general with a view to achieving its general economic objectives. Local authorities are directly responsible for about 25 per cent of public expenditure. Elected local councils, through their appropriate committees are responsible for the major part of expenditure on education, police, housing and other environmental services.

In recent years the Government has indicated that it believes that there is scope for significant reductions in local authority current and capital expenditure without jeopardising reasonable service standards. The Government's political opponents argue that this position is an aspect of the Conservative Party's market agenda and that the shift in emphasis away from local authority provision is really part of a political programme masquerading as an economic expediency.

Where now the State?

This chapter has outlined the reasons for, and ways in which, the State has become involved directly and indirectly in the provision of housing. It has shown that the rationale for intervention has political, social and economic dimensions.

In the late 1980s the financial arrangements which support this intervention are undergoing a fundamental restructuring. This restructuring has significant implications for the ways in which finance is channelled towards the provision and maintenance of housing. Much of the existing system of housing finance and the projected changes can only be properly appreciated and understood in terms of the tenures in which they operate. For this reason the detailed analysis of the system of housing finance which follows is organised on a tenure basis.

Tighter controls on housing expenditure
Before the Thatcher Administration's systematic efforts to cut back on public sector housing expenditure, the preceding Labour Government attempted to control the programme in a fairly *ad hoc* fashion through the PESC planning system, through the introduction of cash limits in 1976 and through the 'housing cost yardstick' which tied public sector capital costs to fixed limits. In addition, between 1975 and 1977, Section 105 of the Housing Rents and Subsidies Act 1975 was used to impose limits on local authority spending for house acquisition and improvement of the existing stock. House construction in the public sector was restricted through the existing controls on borrowing which were strengthened in 1976.

The measures proved to be inadequate and in 1977 a more comprehensive system of housing investment programmes (HIPs) was introduced.

Housing Investment Programmes[9]
Under the HIPs system each local authority has been required to submit its bid for housing investment for the coming year and these have been collectively considered in the context of total housing needs and national priorities. Allocations have been made out of the sum allowed nationally for expenditure on housing. Initially, the allocation was made under the three spending blocks of (a) local authority investment, (b) improvement grants, and (c) lending to housing associations. In 1979 the new Conservative Government strengthened the HIP system by replacing the three blocks with a single allocation which became the legal limit for housing capital expenditure under the Local Government Planning and Land Act 1980. This legislation might be seen as marking the beginning of a shift away from an era of 'consultation and influence' to an era of 'direction, control and confrontation'.

The era of direction
After 1979 central-local relations experienced a change in emphasis involving a more rigorous attempt by central Government to control the expenditure of local authorities. Much of the machinery of control already existed (e.g. cash limits) and some new machinery was introduced.

The new machinery was established under the provisions of the Local Government Planning and Land Act 1980.

The Local Government Planning and Land Act 1980
The overall effect of this legislation was to enhance the powers of the Secretary of State for the Environment. The Act replaced the Needs and Resources elements of the Rate Support Grant with a new Block Grant. Under this system the Exchequer provides a grant to each local authority based upon a calculation which takes into account both *what the DOE reckons* they need to spend to provide a standard service (the grant-related expenditure) and *what the DOE reckons* is a reasonable burden for local ratepayers to bear (the grant-related poundage). More will be said about this in chapter 5.

The key feature of the revised arrangements is that it allows the Secretary of State to penalise those local authorities deemed to be 'over-spending'. By having the power to set and alter what counts as grant related expenditure his Department has in its power a mechanism which actually *defines* 'over-spending'. What is more, year by year, the detailed arrangements can be altered, thereby altering the definition of 'over-spending'. The system has been used politically by the Secretary of State to identify and label a number of authorities as 'profligate'.

Tightening the screw: The Local Government Finance Act 1982
By 1982 the Secretary of State was arguing that the threat of reducing grant (and in some cases, actual reductions of grant) was not diminishing the 'irresponsible' spending plans of the 'profligate' authorities. Further action was required where authorities protected their services by increasing local taxes to compensate for loss of grant. He considered placing a ceiling on the non-domestic rate charged to businesses, and requiring authorities to hold a referendum before levying supplementary rate increases (i.e. a second rate demand in the course of a year). The referendum idea was opposed within the Conservative Party and was not followed through, but local authority powers to impose supplementary rates were nevertheless abolished by the Local Government Finance Act 1982.

As well as abolishing supplementary rates, the 1982 Act strengthened the Secretary of State's powers of control over 'profligate' authorities by allowing him to reduce the grant to such authorities in the course of a financial year. He could now exert his influence more than once in a year in cases where his Department defined 'over-spending'.

Another turn on the screw: Rate capping
In 1985/86 the Government sought powers in England and Wales to limit the level of general rate levied by selected local authorities.[10] In Scotland selective powers already existed. The idea was to target a relatively small number of authorities whose spending was deemed to be excessive in relation to the block grant formula (grant related expenditure). These were to be given figures for their permitted rate levies, and if they disagreed with the DOE, the Secretary of State could go to Parliament to put the force of law behind the recommendations. In 1985-86, the first eighteen authorities were rate capped.

The future of central–local relations
It is clear that underlying many of the changes imposed on local authorities by the present Conservative Government is an attempt to reformulate the role of local government in a free enterprise economy. Government pronouncements and enactments have created a climate of opinion which points to local authorities having more of an 'enabling' and less of a 'providing' role. In the case of housing this change in emphasis was made quite explicit in the 1987 White Paper *Housing: The Government's Proposals.*

Although this view fits in with the Government's commitment to the 'market agenda', it has met, and undoubtedly will continue to meet, opposition from those who see a local authority as more than a field agency for central government or a managing agent coordinating the private provision of community and welfare services. The fact that there still exists a strong body of opinion that sees a need for social housing to be provided within a context of direct local accountability means that political tensions between central and local government will continue into the future.

Notes and references

1. Since 1978 that part of the capital expenditure of nationalised industries which is financed from internal trading surpluses or from non-governmental external sources, such as domestic borrowing or borrowing from abroad, has not been included in the official measure of public expenditure. The definition now assumes that nationalised industries are best regarded as more or less autonomous.

2. Although tax revenue foregone through mortgage interest tax relief does not officially count as public expenditure, in recent years, the figure has appeared in the Public Expenditure White Paper. In the 1988-89 White Paper, for example, it appeared in Table 6.5 of Volume 1, and showed that the estimated cost of the concession to the Exchequer for the year 1987-88 was £4,750 million. The figure for 1989-90 is expected to be £5,500 million. It is estimated that every 1 per cent rise in interest rates increases MITR by £450 million.

3. Taken from *The Government's Expenditure Plans 1988-89 to 1990-91,* Cm. 288-1, HMSO, January 1988, Table 1.4.

4. The following is based on the glossary of terms in the Expenditure White Paper op.cit., Vol.1, pp.114

5. Figures taken from Cm.288-1 op.cit., 1988, Chart 1.10 and Tables 5.7 and 5.8.

6. Figures taken from *Social Trends,* HMSO 1988, Table 5.6 and 1988 Cm.288-1, Table 6.5.

7. *The Control of Public Expenditure* Cm.1432 (The Plowden Report), HMSO 1961.

8. If the limit is underspent in any one year, the provision for the following year is increased to match the underspend, up to a maximum percentage (currently 5%) of the cash limit of the year in which the underspend occurs (DoE Circulars 6/84 and 9/85 and Welsh Office Circulars 20/84 and 17/85).

9. Refer to DoE Circular 63/77.

10. The idea was put forward in *Rates: Proposals for Rate Limitation and Reform of the Rating System,* Cm.9008, HMSO, August 1983.

Part 2
Capital finance

Chapter 3
Capital and owner occupation

The concept of ownership

A house is not 'owned' in the same way that consumer dura-
bles such as cameras and refrigerators are 'owned'. In purchasing
a house, the owner occupier does not so much gain absolute
possession of the building and the physical land, as acquire a
bundle of legally enforceable *freehold* rights relating to their use
and disposal. This is an important point because it underlines the
fact that others may also 'own' legal rights or interests in the
same property (such as leasehold rights, tenancy rights or rights
of easement). Such legal interests have a market value of their
own and their existence can also affect the market value of the
freehold.

Capital finance and access to owner occupation

Money capital is used to purchase new and second hand houses and
to make improvements and additions to such dwellings. In other words,
for most households, money capital is the key to both gaining access
to owner occupation and to increasing the quality and quantity of
their housing once access has been obtained. Initial access usually
involves either having sufficient money capital for outright purchase
or the taking out of a loan. The acquisition of a loan usually depends
upon a combination of factors: the borrower's income and prospects
of income, and the capacity of the property to act as a sound security
against the advance.

The growth and structure of owner occupation

Owner occupation as a tenure arrangement has expanded continuously throughout this century. Over 60 per cent of Britain's housing stock is now owner occupied, compared with less than 10 per cent in 1914 and about 55 per cent in 1979. However, this figure conceals a very marked social stratification and significant national, regional and local variations. Over 90 per cent of the professional/managerial class are now home-owners compared with less than 30 per cent of unskilled manual workers. Wales has the highest British national level of ownership with 68 per cent of its stock in the hands of occupiers; the proportions for England and Scotland are 66 per cent and 43 per cent respectively. In the regions, the South West has nearly 70 per cent of its stock in owner occupation while the North has only 54 per cent. Variations also exist locally at the district level. In some parts of London, for example, the largest single tenure is private rented; elsewhere, other localities may be almost exclusively owner occupied or dominated by a large council housing estate.

The further expansion of home ownership aimed at by current Government policies will require more buyers to be drawn from lower income groups and from particular regions and areas.

Owner occupation and government policy

The present Government has welcomed and strongly encouraged the growth of owner occupation. This is reflected in the following extract from the 1987 White Paper *Housing: The Government's Proposals* (Cm.214, HMSO September 1987):

> "Clearly, the majority of people wish to own their own homes. This wish should in the Government's view be supported. Home ownership gives people independence; it gives them a sense of greater personal responsibility; and it helps to spread the Nation's wealth more widely. These are important factors in the creation of a more stable and prosperous society. . . . . . ."

The Conservative Party's commitment to expand owner occupation as a 'socially desirable' tenure arrangement is well established. During their period in office from 1970 to 1974 they published the White Paper *Fair Deal for Housing* (Cm.4728. HMSO July 1971). This argued that home ownership satisfies 'a deep and natural desire' in us all, and that, as well as encouraging thrift, the expansion in home ownership would lead to houses being better maintained at less real cost. In this way, it argued that it would be sensible for the Government to encourage the development of the tenure through the use of the fiscal system.

For many years a major objective within the market agenda for housing policy has been the expansion of home-ownership in relation to renting.

Government encouragement of owner occupation has taken a number of forms. These are summarised in Figure 2.3.1.

Fiscal support for owner occupation

Although owner occupiers have access to various grants (see Chapter 5), the tenure is mainly subsidised indirectly through tax concessions rather than directly through cash receipts.

The real economic subsidy to owner occupation is higher than generally understood. Mortgage interest tax relief is popularly perceived as *the way* in which owner occupiers are subsidised: however, the true subsidy is a good deal broader and is composed of three elements:

1. Mortgage interest tax relief relates to the householder's costs of servicing the capital loan taken out to purchase the property. As we explained in Chapter 1, such servicing costs are regarded as part of *revenue* expenditure, and for this reason we will consider them in Chapter 6 which is concerned with the revenue rather than the capital aspects of owning (i.e. the financial aspects of *being* rather than the financial aspects of *becoming* an owner occupier).

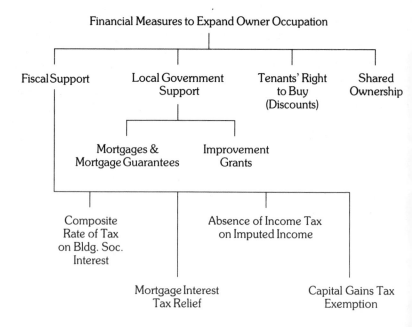

Figure 2.3.1

2. The absence of income taxation on the imputed income derived from home ownership. The notion of a domestic property generating an income for its owner occupier is a complex idea relating to questions of revenue and will be dealt with in Chapter 6.

3. The absence of capital gains taxation in relation to a household's main domestic residence relates to the *capital* gain that may result directly from owner occupation and is dealt with below.

On the basis of this tripartite definition of the subsidy, it can be argued that, for most years, the total subsidy going to owner occupiers is actually in excess of the total planned public expenditure on housing *in all tenures.*[1]

Capital gains

In Chapter 1 we made the point that an owner occupier has an investment as well as a consumption interest in his or her house. An important part of this investment interest relates to the property's potential to be sold for more than it cost to purchase. When this occurs the owner realises a capital gain; when this occurs in relation to his or her main or only domestic residence, this gain is not subject to taxation. This concession contrasts with the treatment of capital gains made on other types of investment including those on second homes and other houses held solely for investment purposes.

The case for taxing owner-occupiers' capital gains can be argued on the grounds of both fairness and efficiency. All capital gains are, strictly speaking, as much a source of income as are wages, dividends and rents, and it is for this reason that they are usually subject to taxation. By specifically excluding from taxation gains stemming from the ownership of a domestic residence, it might be argued that the fiscal system operates inequitably by discriminating in favour of one group of citizens simply on the basis of their housing tenure. It can also be argued that many other capital gains are in fact taxed, and the efficient operation of the capital market requires that all assets be treated more or less equally for fiscal purposes.[2]

The counter argument, in favour of not taxing the owner occupier's capital gains, usually has two elements. The first is political in that it forms part of the 'market agenda' and relates to the Government's desire to use the fiscal system to encourage the growth of owner occupation. The second is based on the proposition that, in contrast to capital gains made on other types of investment (such as stocks and shares), those made on domestic residences are rarely realised. That is, when a house is sold, the owner typically reinvests the gain straightaway in another property. Because of this, it is argued that it is more appropriate for the fiscal system to deal with any capital gain at the end of the owner's life through inheritance tax rather than via capital gains tax at points of sale and repurchase.

Inheritance tax

Forty per cent inheritance tax is currently paid (1989) on estates in excess of £118,000. In recent years, with house prices in some areas rising rapidly, many more families than formally will be drawn into paying inheritance tax. It has been calculated that the surviving families of the 155,000 house owners who currently die each year, receive in total some £6.8 billion of property inheritance.[3] For most people this does not present a particular problem, and is simply a matter of them submitting to the reasonable and established principle of progressive taxation: namely, that an increase in wealth carries with it an increased tax responsibility. There is, however, a potential problem facing one particular group of people.

Where, for example, a middle-aged son or daughter lives at home with a widowed parent, financial difficulties may arise when the parent eventually dies if the family home has to be sold up in order to meet the inheritance tax liability. It used to be possible to solve this problem by the parent transferring the house into the son or daughter's name; this route, however, is now closed. The Inland Revenue now argues that by continuing to live in the house after giving it away, the giver 'reserves a benefit' in the property which makes it still liable as part of the giver's estate. It may be possible to get round this problem by the parent paying a full rent, but this may not be seen to be advisable because of potential security of tenure issues in the case of some future family dispute.

Housing as personal wealth

With about 63 per cent of Britain's housing stock currently owner occupied, dwellings now account for more than 70 per cent of all privately owned assets and just under half of the estimated £1,200 billion of the nation's private wealth. Research has indicated that by the year 2000 more than 202,000 houses will be bequeathed annually to the relatives of deceased householders[4]. This collective inheritance will be worth something like £9 billion a year (in 1986 prices). If it is assumed that in the year 2000 half the families in the nation will not be liable to inherit any property wealth at all, and that of those who do, most will be home owners in their own right, then the inheritors will be double beneficiaries of any real rise in house prices between now and the end of the century. This process has been described as 'familial accumulation'[5] a term which reflects the fact that the housing market is likely to operate in a way that increases the wealth gap between home owning and non-home owning families.

All of this assumes certain demographic trends and also that between now and the year 2000 house prices will increase in line with or ahead of wages and that there are no radical changes in the way in which property wealth is taxed. It may be that a future government will judge that this form of personal wealth accumulation, which does not derive from the productive process, is not in the national interest and will introduce some form of wealth tax or higher rates of inheritance tax as a result. Also, it may be judged that rapid house price inflation is damaging to the economy and in the future a new form of property tax may be introduced in an attempt to restrict house price rises.

House price inflation and the economy
Economists interested in how the housing and labour markets interact, suggest that the rapid house price inflation of recent years, especially in the southeast, has had a detrimental effect on Britain's general economic performance.[6] It is argued that the economic dominance of the southeast of England has led to an expanded need for houses in that region and that the existence of readily available credit has turned this need into effective demand. This demand is increased by favourable tax arrangements and confident expectations that the rise in house prices will continue to outstrip the general rate of inflation. Because of land shortages in the southeast supply cannot easily be increased to meet this extra demand with the consequence that house prices rise still further. The regional house price differential then acts as a disincentive for workers to move into the southeast to fill vacancies and also acts to discourage workers from moving out of the southeast to other parts of the country because they fear that they may not be able to return should the need arise. As well as inhibiting labour mobility, high house prices in the southeast help to create pressure for higher wages and salaries in that region, and some commentators argue that conditions in the southeast have a disproportionate effect on national wage settlements.

By such arguments some economists claim that recent house price increases have led to additional wage cost inflation as well as to problems related to the geographical immobility of labour.

In addition to these problems, it is clear that the Treasury and the Bank of England are also concerned about the extent to which the increases in housing equity which result from house price inflation leak out of the housing system into general consumer spending.

Equity growth and equity leakage
Because the ownership of the value of a property is often complicated by the existence of a mortgage loan and the interests of a lender (mortgagee), the question of capital gains is sometimes considered in relation to the idea of 'equity growth'. For the freeholder with a mortgage, his or her 'equity' is represented by *that part of the property's market value which is in excess of all debts to which it is liable.* In recent years, house price inflation has produced a situation in which many owner occupiers have experienced a rapid growth in the equity which is tied up in their houses.

As indicated above, one rationale for exempting owner occupiers from capital gains tax is the argument that, so long as they stay in owner occupation, any equity growth remains locked into their houses and is only unlocked by death, emigration or change of tenure. However, this assumption is clearly false: a great deal of equity is withdrawn from the housing system by owners who are not last-time sellers. As house prices have increased, 'house rich/cash poor' owners have developed a number of strategies for unlocking part of their equity, and it is clear that the Bank of England and the Treasury recognize that, in recent years, the conversion of housing value into cash has helped to fuel a general rise in the level of consumer spending. Such withdrawals are most easily achieved at the point of sale and repurchase by a process of 'trading up' or 'trading down' the market. In this way, some owners in mid-housing career trade up with a mortgage which is larger than that needed to purchase the new property; and numbers of older owners are increasingly acquiring extra money for their retirement by moving and trading down to less expensive houses. In addition, the commercial banks have recently developed various 'equity release' schemes which allow owners whose houses have appreciated in value to unlock some of this gain for some consumer purpose such as the purchase of a new car.

House price inflation is double sided: the capital appreciation it creates can be seen as a financial benefit to existing owners or as a financial burden, or even a barrier, to those seeking entry to the tenure. The housing system has reacted to the problem of access by producing such arrangements as low-start mortgages, and shared ownership schemes (see below).

As well as fiscal stimuli, over the years, governments have utilised local authority arrangements to encourage the growth of owner occupation (refer Figure 2.3.1).

Local government support: loans, loan guarantees and voluntary shared ownership schemes

Loans and Loan Guarantees
As early as 1923 the Chamberlain Act allowed local authorities to grant mortgages and mortgage guarantees to individuals who found difficulty in acquiring building society finance. The ability of local authorities to make advances or guarantee the repayments to building societies of any advances they made, was further reinforced by the Housing (Financial Provisions) Act 1959, as amended by the House Purchase and Housing Act 1959. Table 2.3.1 indicates that during 1975 local authority lending was exceptionally high at a time when there was a shortage of building society funds. After 1976, however, local authority mortgages became more restricted and currently they contribute an insignificant amount to the total provision of house purchase finance.

Shared ownership

In addition to the common arrangement of joint ownership by (say) man and wife, there are three broad categories of 'shared ownership': 'traditional shared ownership', 'co-ownership' and 'joint purchase'.

1. Traditional Shared Ownership This involves a relationship between a single owner and some recognized housing agency, such as a housing association, local authority or new town.

A common route to traditional shared ownership is via the schemes run by local authorities and housing associations which typically involve the housing agency acquiring a suitable property on the open market and subsequently selling on a part share of the equity in the house to the household. Thus, under these schemes, the agency retains some proportion of the equity of a dwelling with the occupier owning the remainder of the property's value in the form of a long lease. The occupier's stake is usually acquired by means of a mortgage loan from some financial institution such as a building society with experience of shared ownership purchases or from the agency landlord. In addition to repaying the principal and interest on the mortgage, the occupier is liable to pay rent on that part of the property retained by the agency. Should the occupier wish to move, two broad options become available. Firstly, he or she can purchase the equity share belonging to the agency prior to selling the house at the prevailing market value: this effectively takes the house out of shared ownership. Secondly, the occupier's existing share can be sold back to the agency. In either case, the occupier receives a proportion of the proceeds related to his or her equity stake at the point of resale.

Because equity sharing is specifically designed as a mechanism for encouraging owner occupation, schemes usually allow owners to increase their initial shares as and when they can afford to do so: this arrangement is sometimes termed 'staircasing'. In this way they may, by stages, become full owners. In cases where the landlord agency owns the freehold, it is normally transferred to the occupier as soon as he or she has purchased a 100 per cent interest. In the case of flats, it is possible that the occupier may not gain the freehold but instead acquire the right to a long lease at a nominal rent as soon as he or she becomes the full owner.

2. Co-ownership Until 1974 the Housing Corporation provided funds for a number of co-ownership societies or 'equity co-operatives'. Some still operate but the Corporation no longer funds such arrangements. These schemes involved a relationship between a specialist co-ownership housing society and a group of people who constituted its members. The primary function of the society or association was to provide housing for the membership. The principle of this form of arrangement was that the members purchased their houses by means of a combination of Housing Corporation and building society loans which were negotiated and administered by the society. When members move from a co-ownership house they take with them a lump sum representing the increased equity in the individual dwelling.

3. Joint purchase This involves an arrangement by which two or more potential owner occupiers come together jointly to purchase a dwelling. The most straightforward scheme, involving the legal minimum, simply requires all the owners having their names on the deeds. Experience has shown, however, that such a minimalist arrangement can be fraught with danger, and can lead to lengthy disputes if and when one of the parties wants to move or make some physical change to the land or buildings. To overcome such problems, it is sometimes recommended that the parties set up a trust in the form of an agreement that spells out what the parties will do under various circumstances. Other, more complicated arrangements are also possible. Where, for example, the parties wish jointly to convert (say) a large, run-down property, it might be advisable to set up a corporate body, such as a housing cooperative, for the purpose. This would involve keeping accounts which have to be audited annually and sent to the Registrar of Friendly Societies.

Tenants' right to buy[7]

Under recent Conservative Administrations another method of extending owner occupation has come to the fore: namely, the privatisation of public sector housing via a policy to enable and encourage local authority and housing association tenants to buy their houses at discounted prices.

Tenants' 'right to buy' (RTB) their houses at discounts of up to 50 per cent was the centrepiece of the Housing Act 1980. Subsequent legislation in the form of the 1986 Housing and Planning Act, made the RTB discounts even more attractive and, in addition, made it possible for councils to designate estates to be offered for sale *en bloc* to private trusts or developers.

Under the legislation, most secure tenants (as defined in the Housing Act 1980) of district councils, London borough councils, new town development corporations, non-charitable housing associations, and certain other bodies (such as some set up as a result of the abolition of the Greater London Council and the metropolitan councils), have the right to buy the homes they inhabit. This right is dependent on them being secure tenants of a housing agency identified by the legislation as a RTB landlord. In addition they must normally have had to have spent a total of at least two years as a tenant of their present landlord or of some other RTB landlord or as a member of the regular armed forces occupying service accommodation.

The right to buy is restricted to houses or flats which are rented as separate dwellings and are occupied as the tenant's only or main home. Any member of the same family who holds a joint tenancy can participate in the purchase, and in addition, the purchaser may share the RTB with up to three members of his or her family who are not joint tenants provided the property is the main home of all of them.

Some properties such as almshouses, specially adapted housing, certain dwellings let by charitable housing agencies and housing co-operatives, properties on land which has been acquired for development and various types of tied accommodation are excluded from the RTB provisions. In some areas local authorities have developed 'transferable discount' schemes, enabling tenants of dwellings in these restricted categories who wish to exercise their right to buy, to take advantage of the discount in conjunction with the purchase of some other non-restricted property. Such a property may be in local authority or housing association ownership. (The RTB regulations are more fully explained in the DOE/Welsh Office booklet 'Your right to buy your home' (1987).

The discount may be up to £35,000 and is based on the person's 'qualifying period' of tenancy. The applicant must have a qualifying period of at least two years and the basic discount after this minimum period is 32 per cent for houses and 44 per cent for flats. Currently (1989), these discounts rise to a maximum of 60 per cent for houses and 70 per cent for flats after 15 years of tenancy.

The legislation includes a special *cost floor* rule which prevents RTB discounts from reducing the purchase price below the amount spent since the end of March 1974 on acquiring, building or improving the property. In the 1987 White Paper the Government said it intended to abolish the cost floor rule, but strong representations from the housing lobby argued that abolition would act as a disincentive to authorities and associations making future capital investment decisions. In the event, the new legislation modified rather than abolished the rule, and the new Act said that in future, costs incurred within the last eight years before the sale should be taken into account in calculating the cost floor. In Scotland, where the cost floor cut-off is currently December 1978, the Government has said that only costs incurred within five years before the sale can be taken into account.

To date the RTB legislation has had the effect of transferring about one fifth of the public sector stock into owner occupation (over a million tenants). Much of this transfer has involved higher-quality property and better-off tenants. Selling high-rise flats has proved to be difficult with fewer than one in ten changing hands. It would appear that the original thrust of the 1980 initiative is running out of steam, and in the early summer of 1988 rumours of a new 'transfer initiative' appeared in the press. These related to proposals associated with Peter Walker, the then Secretary of State for Wales, and centred on the notion of a 'buy-as-you-rent' scheme which would allow tenants to qualify for the RTB discounts by putting down a small deposit with a building society or housing association and then paying rent as a mortgage. Under this plan, some 4.5 million council tenants could cease to pay rent and instead pay the same amount, inflation-linked, in mortgage payments until they would become full owners. If they then decided to sell their homes, they would be able to realize the value of their free stakes which could then be used as a down-payments on other houses.

Sources of house purchase finance

In this concluding section we will consider the nature of mortgage finance and the institutions involved in its provision.

Mortgages

Houses that are not inherited or bought outright are usually acquired by means of a loan. Where the property itself is used as security for the repayment, the loan is popularly referred to as a *mortgage*. Strictly speaking the 'mortgage' is the legal agreement which gives the lender rights over the property if the borrower defaults on the loan. Because with mortgage arrangements the house is pledged as security, the lender retains the title deeds until the loan is repaid.

Types of mortgages: repayment mortgages
The most straightforward type of house purchase loan is the repayment mortgage: this is sometimes referred to as an annuity mortgage. This involves the borrower making monthly payments to the lender, partly of interest on the outstanding loan and partly of capital to repay the loan. In the early years, most of the monthly payment goes to paying off the interest, but as the outstanding loan is gradually repaid, the interest element reduces and eventually the major part of the payment is used to repay the capital. The actual monthly payment will depend upon the size of the loan, the length of the repayment period (known as the 'term'), and the current rate of interest. The typical arrangement involves a *level payment mortgage* which requires the repayment of a fixed monthly sum that only varies with changes in the rate of interest. However, some lenders offer *low start repayment mortgages* which are technically known as 'gross profile mortgages'. With such an arrangement the monthly payments are lower in the early years of the term but gradually increase each year, so that during the latter years they are higher than they would otherwise have been with an ordinary repayment mortgage. These loans are designed for people who, at the time of taking out the loan, are on a tight budget but have expectations of a rising income: over the full term of the loan, such arrangements are usually more expensive than conventional repayment mortgages. Should the mortagor die during mortgage term, the payments will still need to be paid to the mortgagee or the total balance outstanding repaid. To protect the interests of the mortgagor's dependants from the financial consequences of such an eventuality, it is usually possible to take out a mortgage protection policy with an insurance company. Similar protection is also given by means of an endowment mortgage.

Endowment mortgages
The principle of an endowment mortgage is that the loan is linked to an insurance policy which matures at the end of the loan term. During the term, the borrower only pays interest to the lender, together with a premium to the insurer, and the capital is then repaid at the end of the mortgage term using the proceeds of the matured policy. The endowment

policy is deposited with the lending institution throughout the duration of the mortgage. There are various types of endowment mortgage, all with built-in life cover but with somewhat differing arrangements and potential benefits.

Low cost endowment mortgages
A low cost endowment mortgage is designed to keep the monthly payments to a minimum and brings together a term assurance policy which will repay the loan should the mortgagor die prematurely and an investment-type endowment insurance policy to produce a sum of money on maturity which should be enough to pay off the debt at that time. It may in addition, provide a cash lump sum over and above the debt liability.

Endowment policies are 'portable' and the policy holders are able to 'take them with them' when they move house. In individual instances, however, more expensive policies may be needed to cover larger loans where lenders do not accept a mixture of endowment and repayment mortgages in such circumstances.

Under a normal low cost endowment the premiums payable are the same each month. Some companies offer *low start low cost endowments* which allow the premium payments to be reduced in the early years.

Full endowment mortgage with profits
A full endowment mortgage operates in a similar way to the low cost model, but the life cover is provided entirely by an endowment policy rather than partly by a term assurance. As well as guaranteeing a sum to pay off the loan, the policy incorporates a savings scheme which produces a sum of money at the end of the term which may be significantly greater than that needed to cover the debt. This is done by bonuses being added to the initial sum assured so that at the end of the term, the policy holder should receive a lump sum over and above the mortgage loan repayment.

The way it works is that the company regularly credits the policy with 'reversionary' bonuses and on maturity with a 'terminal' bonus: the size of these is determined by the profits which the insurance company makes by investing the premium payments. Once declared and added, the bonuses cannot be removed: they will add to the value of the policy and 'revert' to the policy holder at the end of the term. The company will only take into account the reversionary bonuses when calculating the amount needed to cover and repay the mortgage, and the terminal bonus acts as a sort of 'safety buffer' which then guarantees that the loan will be (more than) repaid.

Unit linked mortgages
Compared with ordinary with profits policies, these schemes have a greater element of risk associated with them: their values will tend to fluctuate with the stock market. They operate in a similar way to low cost endowment assurances in that the cash sum produced by the policy at maturity is credited to the mortgage account and any surplus

is then paid to the policy holder. The savings element of the policy is channelled into an investment fund by the purchase of 'units'. The fund may deal in British or overseas property and stocks and shares, and the value of the units will fluctuate in line with how the fund prospers. The cash amount at maturity will be dependent upon the value of all of the units held at that time. The company may sometimes review the value of the units to ensure that they are increasing at a rate sufficient to repay the mortgage, and if they are not, they may request additional premiums in order to acquire further units. If the value of the policy matches the mortgage debt at a time prior to the maturity date, the policy holder may choose to repay the mortgage at that time: in this way, unit linked schemes provide an additional element of flexibility over other endowment schemes.

Pension linked mortgages.
These schemes are usually aimed at the self-employed or people who do not belong to a company pension scheme. The principle involves building up a fund that will repay the loan as well as provide the policy holder with a retirement pension. They work in a way which is similar to that of 'with profits endowments', but instead of an endowment policy, the mortgagor takes out a retirement annuity which, as well as providing a pension, pays a lump sum on retirement (or thereabouts) which is intended to pay off the mortgage. As contributions attract tax relief at the individual's marginal tax rate and are invested in funds that accumulate on a gross basis, free of all taxes, these schemes are particularly tax efficient and therefore attractive to high earners who are eligible to join them. However, by the provisions of the Finance Act (No. 2) 1987, the Inland Revenue has imposed limits on the amount of tax free benefit on such schemes, including an absolute limit of £150,000 per arrangement.

Because of the tax advantages, pension mortgages have been popular with high earning executives and self employed groups who have considerable control over their own pension arrangements, but, until recently, they have not been widely available to employees in company schemes. Pension managers have tended to take a rather paternalistic attitude and argue that it is not in an employee's interest to reduce a pension entitlement to pay off a mortgage. However, with the introduction of radical new pension arrangements in 1988 and the consequential intensification of competition in the pension plans market, attitudes are changing.

The Government's 'Homeloan' scheme

This scheme was introduced under the provisions of the Home Purchase Assistance and Housing Corporation Guarantee Act 1978 and is designed to give some financial assistance to first-time purchasers buying with a mortgage loan from a recognised lending institution. It is really a government sponsored *savings scheme* aimed at encouraging would-be owners to enter the tenure.

The scheme provides special government assistance in the form of an extra loan (£600 currently, 1988), interest-free for up to five years together with a tax-free bonus up to a specified limit (currently £110). The help applies throughout Britain but is only available to people buying low-priced homes. The Government fixes, and periodically changes, price limits for each region in England, Wales, Scotland and Northern Ireland.

To gain the bonus the prospective purchaser has to give notice to his or her savings institution that they wish to join the scheme and the institution has to agree to the arrangement. The depositor then has to save for at least two consecutive years and must have accumulated a specified sum (currently £300) one full year before applying for the bonus. The higher the level of savings maintained throughout that year the larger will be the final tax free bonus granted. An additional requirement has to be met in order to qualify for the extra loan: namely, the saver must have a specified sum (currently £600) in his or her account when applying for benefits. If this condition is met the Government then pays the saver the extra loan through the institution providing the mortgage. Although the extra loan is added to the mortgage, the borrower will not normally have to start repayments or pay any interest on this element of his or her debt for five years.

The changing nature of the mortgage market

Since 1980 it is possible to detect two broad categories of change affecting the mortgage market. One relates to increased competition and the appearance of new providers of house purchase finance and the other relates to the development of a wider product range.

In the 1970s the market was dominated by the building societies who regularly provided up to 90 per cent of lending in any one year. In the early 1980s the commercial banks together with a number of specialised mortgage institutions entered the market and for a time annexed over 40 per cent of the market. By the late 1980s the market stabilised with the societies providing about 60 per cent and the banks a little over 35 per cent of total lending.

An aspect of the new competitive environment has been an increasing tendency to respond in a more flexible way to the particular needs of borrowers. In the 1970s the institutions tended to see themselves as providing a fairly standard product to a fairly typical group of borrowers. This typification can be characterised as a twenty five year repayment or endowment loan to young or middle-aged couples in secure employment wishing to acquire a not-too-dilapidated detached or semi-detached house in a not-too-run-down area. The institutions now see themselves as providing a much wider service and a non-standard product. They have become aware that they are operating in a market where people do not simply leave home in order to marry, and single people form a substantial group of borrowers; where lower income people have expectations to become owners, and where retired people wish to take out new mortgages for specialised housing.

The lending institutions

New entrants into the owner occupied market acquire their houses by means of inheritances, savings, gifts or loans. The lump sum necessary to acquire the asset and cover the transaction and relocation costs may, of course, be assembled from more than one source.

Table 2.3.1 Mortgage Lending: Net Advances (%)

Year	Building Societies	Banks	Local Authorities	Insurance Companies	Other
1970	87	3	6	3	1
1975	76	2	17	2	3
1980	80	7	6	5	2
1981	68	24	3	3	2
1982	58	36	4	n	2
1983	75	24	−2	1	2
1984	85	12	−1	1	3
1985	77	22	−3	1	3
1986	74	18	−2	1	9
1987	52	34	−1	3	12
1988*	60	26	−1	3	12

n = less than 0.5%
* = provisional

Source: based on Table T3.3 Bristol & West Building Society, *Factual Background*, Autumn 1987. p. 18.

Table 2.3.1 indicates that building societies and banks are by far the most important source of mortgage finance. The table also shows that after 1981 banks began to make a significant contribution to the total provision of home loans, and have, since that date, been an important but volatile influence in the mortgage market. It also shows that local authorities and insurance companies have played an insignificant part in the market in recent years. Some twenty insurance companies have mortgage funds to lend, and they are also a source of top-up loans when a first mortgage offer is insufficient to meet a purchaser's needs. Local authority mortgages played a significant part for a short period after the return of a Labour Government in 1974. They were usually given for older properties for which traditional mortgage finance was not so readily available. Council funds are now severely limited since the Government restricts the amount they lend through the Housing Investment Programme process. Table 2.3.1 shows that net advances (i.e. taking into account repayments) for local authorities were negative between 1983 and 1986, reflecting the fact that they were receiving more in repayments than granting in the form of new mortgages.

The traditional distinction between building societies and banks
The commercial banks are public limited companies operating under the auspices of the Registrar of Companies. They are owned by shareholders whose shares are quoted on the Stock Exchange. Traditionally, building societies have operated in a separate financial sector. Since the first comprehensive Building Societies Act in 1874, they have been treated as mutual co-operative organisations set apart from the controls and regulations of the banks and other commercial finance institutions. Their special legal powers were derived from a succession of statutes which were consolidated into the Building Societies Act 1962 which recognised their mutual, non-profit-making nature by requiring their overall supervision to be administered by the Registrar of Friendly Societies.

The societies have traditionally secured the bulk of their funds in the 'small savers' market by issuing shares to investors. Although shares confer membership of the society, they are not transferable and are therefore not comparable with shares in a public company. Normally the investor is issued with a passbook in which is recorded the share value standing to his or her credit. This can be added to or withdrawn from with little fuss and at immediate or short notice. Some societies also offer 'bond' or 'term' shares which have to be held for a specific fixed period in order to obtain a higher rate of interest. Members who hold shares have voting rights in relation to elections to its board of directors.

As well as receiving money from investing members, societies may, subject to the provisions of the Statutes, receive deposits and borrow money from other sources. Depositors who are not members do not have voting rights but do have a prior claim on the assets should the society be wound up.

Concern about the financial instability resulting from the unwise use of funds for property speculation by a few societies after the Second World War led to the imposition of various restraints on building society activities. The 1962 legislation required building societies to concentrate their lending in the form of mortgages and it prevented them from offering the range of financial services provided by the clearing banks. Because mortgages involved them lending over relatively long periods while taking deposits which could be withdrawn at short notice, care was taken to underpin both their general financial stability and their short run liquidity. They were required to hold a proportion of their total assets, prescribed by the Registrar, in the form of cash and gilt-edged or local authorities securities. They were also obliged to hold a proportion of securities with a fairly short maturity date so that, if necessary, liquid funds could be realised to cover any abnormal level of withdrawals with a minimum risk of capital loss.

The changing structure and role of building societies

As we have seen, the institutions playing the most dominant part in the mortgage market are the building societies. Essentially they have acted as financial intermediaries standing between the savings market and the housing system. In this position they have channelled funds from savers to borrowers, and in so doing have played a crucial part in the striking increase in owner occupation that has taken place since the end of the Second World War. The significance of their historical role in this respect is well illustrated by the dramatic increase in building society assets, which have risen from £60 million in 1900 to over £150,000 million in 1989.

With their growing importance the societies have tended to become bigger and fewer in number. By the mid 1980s, the five largest societies controlled 56 per cent of total assets (compared with 45 per cent in 1960). As part of this tendency, the larger societies have developed nationwide branch networks and have become less orientated towards a particular region or locality.

Table 2.3.2 shows a continuous reduction in the number of registered societies: this reflects the fact that over time many small societies have been taken over by larger organisations and also, that in recent years, some of the larger societies have merged. With the passing of two major pieces of reforming legislation in 1986 (see below), this process is likely

Table 2.3.2 Building society trends: Great Britain

Year	Registered Societies No.	Savers' Accounts '000	Borrowers' Accounts '000
1960	726	4,481	2,349
1965	605	6,454	2,845
1970	481	10,883	3,655
1975	382	18,593	4,397
1980	273	31,551	5,383
1981	253	34,383	5,490
1982	227	37,701	5,646
1983	206	38,911	5,928
1984	190	40,930	6,315
1985	167	42,145	6,657
1986	151	43,413	7,025
1987	138	45,800	7,200

Sources: based on The Building Societies Association, *Building Society News*, Vol. 7 No. 1, January 1987, and Bristol & West Building Society, *Factual Background*, Autumn 1987.

to continue into the 1990s. Whilst the number of societies has declined, the number of branches has steadily increased from about 2,000 in 1970 to some 7,000 in 1988.

The common features of building societies and banks
In a housing context building societies and banks can be thought of as playing a similar role: namely, they act as financial intermediaries bridging the savings and mortgage markets.

However, the distinction between building societies and banks has become increasingly blurred. In recent years the societies have begun offering a range of financial services formerly the province of banking institutions. As deposit-takers building societies have traditionally been regarded as savings institutions and their share and deposit accounts have been regarded as safe and accessible refuges for money balances which depositors wish to accumulate and keep for some future use such as the deposit on a house or on a holiday. However, the larger societies are now offering a range of banking-type facilities which have led to deposits with them being increasingly used as *transactions* rather than *savings* balances. The most significant developments have been the linking of building society deposits to instant access accounts with cheque book and cheque guarantee card facilities and the provision of high street cash points. In parallel with these developments, the banks have greatly expanded, and aggressively advertised, their mortgage lending facilities. It can be argued that banks and building societies are now competing in the same markets both as lenders and deposit-takers.

In line with their growing functional similarities, building societies and banks are now treated on a more equal basis by the Inland Revenue. Up to 1984, the *composite tax* arrangement applied exclusively to building societies, but under Section 27 of the Finance Act of that year, it now also applies to banks. Under this arrangement, investors pay no basic rate income tax on interest accruing to bank or building society deposits: instead, a roughly equivalent amount of taxation is levied directly from the institutions. Every year the Inland Revenue carries out a spot check on a sample of savers throughout the country, and then averages out the rates at which they pay tax. The result is known as the *composite rate*, and this rate is then applied to the total interest paid by each bank or society who use it to deduct tax from the interest they pay to depositors. Because some investors in the sample are retired or out of work and pay no income tax, the composite rate invariably works out to be less than the basic rate of income tax. The composite rate for 1989/90, for example, worked out to be 21.75 per cent compared with standard rate income tax of 25 per cent.[8].

The growth of competition
The extension of composite tax arrangements to banks is an indication of the Government's wish for there to be a more common treatment of banks and building societies with regard to their function as deposit-takers.

Recent years have also witnessed a significant shift towards more competition between the societies themselves. The most prominent manifestation of this shift has been the recent breaking up of the so-called 'building societies cartel'. The cartel arrangements which operated in the 1970s involved the Building Societies Association setting recommended rates of interest for both savers and borrowers. The arrangement was 'official' in that it operated with government approval and thereby became exempted from the provisions of the Monopolies and Mergers Act 1976 which is legislation designed to prevent restrictive practices. Over time the cartel was criticised from within and without the movement, and in any event, by the end of the decade, market pressures were undermining the arrangements. The cartel was gradually dismantled in the early 1980s.

By 1981 (see Table 2.3.1) the societies were also experiencing serious competition from the clearing banks in the field of mortgage provision. The societies tended to charge higher rates of interest on their more substantial loans, while the banks tended to offer flat rate mortgages whatever the size of the advance. Because of this, the banks made significant inroads into the more expensive end of the housing market, and this in turn encouraged the societies to liberalise their attitudes to lending on 'down market' properties.

The Building Societies Act 1986

Despite their attempts to respond to external competition, the 1962 legislation prevented the building societies from competing effectively with rival institutions in the banking and insurance sectors. They were, for example, prohibited from offering overdraft facilities and cheque guarantee cards on their newly introduced cheque book accounts; in addition they were only permitted to offer insurance services in conjunction with a mortgage loan.

Both the 1984 Green Paper *Building Societies: A New Framework* (Cm.9316) and the BSA's own discussion paper published a year earlier[9] argued that, while societies should remain mutual finance organisations, they should be allowed a wider range of powers in order to meet the growing competition from the banks and other institutions. The consultation process eventually led to a major piece of reforming legislation in the form of the Building Societies Act 1986. This Act repealed all previous legislation regulating building societies and the majority of its provisions came into force on 1 January 1987.

Under the Act building societies are given the choice of two distinct courses of development. They can either remain as mutual societies with additional powers or they can convert into public limited companies (plc's) subject to the Banking Act 1987.

Conversion into Public Limited Companies (plc's)

The transfer regulations require at least 20 per cent of members to participate in the poll, and of those, at least 75 per cent must favour conversion. A simple majority of borrowers is also required. Members are given priority share purchase rights in the new company.

An institution taking this step ceases to be supervised by the Building Societies Commission and, indeed, is no longer able to call itself a building society. It becomes subject to banking and company law, regulation and taxation. In July 1989 the Abbey National became the first society to abandon its mutual status and become a public company.

Mutual societies with additional powers
Those that choose to remain as building societies are required to retain as their primary purpose the raising of funds for lending on the security of a mortgage to borrowers wishing to purchase owner occupied dwellings. These loans constitute the bulk of the societies' assets. Before 1987 their remaining assets had to be in the form of their own office premises, or a range of prescribed non-speculative and relatively liquid assets authorised by the Chief Registrar of Friendly Societies. Under the new Act, 90 per cent of their lending must still be in the form of mortgage loans, but they now have powers to lend and invest more widely.

The new powers enable the societies to engage in a wider range of commercial activities which can be broadly summarised as follows.

1. The raising of wholesale funds, i.e. deposits of a relatively large denomination placed with the societies by large firms and institutions.
2. The provision of a fuller range of personal banking services. Now they have more power to make unsecured loans, the societies can more readily offer financial services such as credit cards and transmission accounts.
3. The provision of an integrated house buying service including estate agency, surveys, valuations and conveyancing.
4. The power to act as agents for other organisations by making or receiving payments, managing mortgage investments or acting as land managers.
5. The power to establish and manage personal equity plans and personal pension schemes and offer advice on insurance.
6. The right to operate in the EEC through subsidiaries.

Other proposed amendments currently being considered (1989) include the power to offer life insurance, manage their own unit trust funds, provide stock-broking facilities, and extend their ability to make unsecured loans.

The 1986 reforms represent fundamental changes and will enable building societies to take a more active role in the housing system by extending their activities beyond the traditional functions of taking deposits and making mortgage loans. Their new powers mean that some larger societies will now take on development functions and also provide estate management services: some will operate partnership arrangements with local authorities and housing associations in rented or shared ownership schemes; and many will provide a more comprehensive house purchase package embracing estate agency, surveying, valuation and legal services.

The Act imposes certain restrictions on the nature and scope of building society assets. Such assets are now divided into three broad categories:

1. First mortgages on wholly owner occupied residential dwellings.

These are known as 'Class 1' assets and currently, societies are required to keep at least 90 per cent of their total commercial assets in this form.

It is being proposed that this limit on Class 1 assets be cut to 75 per cent by 1993.

2. Other forms of wholly secured lending, such as mortgages on non-residential property, second mortgages.

    This class of loan is known as 'Class 2' assets and must not make up more than 10 per cent of the society's total commercial assets.

3. New activities in the form of higher risk assets such as unsecured loans, ownership of land and equity investment in subsidiaries such as insurance business and estate agency.

    These are known as 'Class 3' assets and are restricted to societies with reserves of more than £3 million: currently they must not constitute more than 5 per cent of total assets.

At present, Class 2 and Class 3 assets must together not constitute more than 10 per cent of total assets, but the limits are to be progressively relaxed to allow a higher proportion of higher risk activities: by January 1993 the relevant proportions will be 25 per cent for non-Class 1 assets and 15 per cent for Class 3 assets.

The supervision of building societies

As well as extending the powers of building societies, the 1986 legislation established a new supervisory framework. The supervision of societies operates under the auspices of the Building Societies Commission (BSC) which is specifically charged with the responsibility of ensuring that the societies operate in the interests of their members and depositors. The BSC is required to administer the regulatory system established by the Act in a way that promotes financial stability, and it is expected to advise Government departments on any matters relating to building societies. The Commission is chaired by the Registrar of Friendly Societies.

In addition to this primary regulatory framework, the societies are subject to some of the provisions of the Financial Services Act 1986 which is designed to extend investor protection in the UK by requiring all institutions (or their agents) conducting investment business to be authorised to do so by the Securities and Investment Board Ltd (SIB), which is to operate with delegated powers from the Secretary of State for Trade and Industry.

Schedule 1 of the Financial Services Act has a fairly broad definition of investment business which includes the giving of financial advice as well as activities associated with direct financial dealings. Many of the additional powers currently granted to societies under schedule 8 of the Building Societies Act are captured by this definition and, if in the future their powers to operate in direct financial dealings are extended, they will become more and more subject to the controls established by the Financial Services Act.

The SIB is financed by a levy (fees) system and is charged with the responsibility of cultivating high standards of solvency, honesty and competence in the financial services sector. In an attempt to prevent it developing into a large and unwieldy bureaucracy, it is intended to recognize five Self-Regulatory Organizations (SROs) to cover such activities as share dealing, financial and commodity futures and options, life assurance and unit trust marketing, and investment management.

Notes and references

1.   O'Sullivan A., *Investment in housing in the UK* in *Inquiry into British Housing: Supplement,* NFHA, July 1986, p. 40.
2.   This point is made by Andrew Walker in *Housing Taxation: Owner Occupation and the Reform of Housing Finance.* CHAS Occasional Paper 9. The Catholic Housing Aid Society, 1986, p. 58. However, apart from the owner occupier's only or main residence, some other assets are exempt from capital gains taxation. These include private motor vehicles, household goods and personal effects up to a fixed limit and most life assurance policies. As well as these exemptions, individuals are allowed a certain amount of gains each year free of tax.
3.   Morgan Grenfell, Housing Inheritance and Wealth in *Economic Review* No. 45, November 1987.
4.   Ibid.
5.   Ibid.
6.   For example, recent press reports pointed to the suggestion that Treasury officials have been deeply impressed by a major study by Oxford Univeristy's Centre for Economic and Policy Research which sets out the extent to which rocketing house prices and the rising differential between house prices in the Southeast and the rest of the country are seriously disrupting the entire economy. (*The Sunday Times,* 10 July 1988).
7.   Much of the following detail is based on the booklet, *Your Right to Buy Your Home: A Guide for Council, New Town and Housing Association Tenants,* DoE/Welsh Office, 1987.
8.   It is important to note that the composite rate arrangement works to the disadvantage of non-tax payers. This is because on all of their investments (except SAYE monthly savings schemes) interest is paid as described, *after* tax has been deducted, and non-tax payers cannot claim a refund. According to the 1987 Family Expenditure Survey, there were some 19 million non-tax payers in 1986 in the UK, of whom 8.6 million were adults and 4 million were retired. Between them, these non-tax payers had something like £14 billion invested with building societies alone.
9.   The John Spalding Report, *The Future Constitution and Powers of Building Societies,* BSA, January 1983.

Chapter 4
Capital finance and the independent rented sector

Access to rented housing

Not everyone has the ability to muster the financial resources necessary to enable them to move into owner-occupation. Access to owner-occupation is regulated by constraints which are specific to the owner-occupied sector, and do not apply to rented housing. Most owner occupiers buy their homes with the help of mortgage finance. The financial institutions which lend to prospective house buyers like to ensure that their borrowers are in reasonably secure employment, that they earn enough to enable them to meet the cost of the loan repayments, and that the property they wish to buy is in good enough condition to retain its capital value throughout the period of the loan.

In the case of rented housing, landlords may make informal inquiries about the income and status of prospective tenants to satisfy themselves that the rent will be paid regularly. Rent is then paid in accordance with a contract between landlord and tenant, on a periodic basis, in return for the use of the accommodation.

It has generally cost less to enter and remain in rented housing than to enter and remain in owner occupation. People who have a low priority for local authority housing, or who do not qualify for admission to local authority waiting lists may find they have to rely on other forms of rented housing. Consequently, rented housing in the 'non-municipal' sector is sometimes the last resort, not only for those who are excluded from the priviliged owner-occupied sector, but also for those who do not have access to local authority housing. Those groups which have come to rely on non-municipal rented housing include the poor, the young, and the mobile population. In the case of housing associations, a wide range of special needs are also catered for.

The structure of the independent rented sector

The Government's 1987 White Paper on housing[1] referred to the non-municipal sphere of rented housing provision as the independent rented sector, grouping together two hitherto distinctly separate tenure sectors. Housing owned by private landlords is closely allied to the market ideology discussed in Chapter 1. In contrast, housing owned by housing associations has, from the birth of the movement been associated with the principles of welfare provision. Private landlords are independent of government, in the sense that they receive no Exchequer support or direct public subsidies. Housing associations on the other hand were and still are substantially dependent upon government for the financing of their operations, though with the increasing importance of private sector finance to the development of their activity, this relationship of 'dependence', along with the broadly social aims of the movement, has been re-examined by politicians and practitioners alike.

The 1988 Housing Act has substantially reformed the structure of the independent rented sector, with the establishment of two main forms of tenancy for the use of private landlords and housing associations alike — the assured tenancy, and the assured shorthold tenancy — and the introduction of provisions designed to phase out tenancies protected under the terms of the Rent Acts[2].

Assured tenancies
Assured tenancies, which in their initial form were governed by the 1954 Landlord and Tenant Act, were extended to residential property by the 1980 Housing Act. They were designed to encourage private landlords who were registered and approved by the Department of the Environment to provide new 'purpose built' accommodation for rent. In return, landlords were free to set rents at market levels, rather than be governed by statutory rent controls.

The 1988 Housing Act has made the assured tenancy the centrepiece of its reforms. Private landlords no longer register with the DoE; assured tenancies cover not only new build, but all types of dwellings; and since assured tenancies entitle landlords to collect market rents, the rent controls contained within the Rent Acts no longer apply. There have in addition been modifications to tenants' rights to security of tenure[3].

These measures from the private landlords' point of view are about removing barriers to private renting, and from the Government's view are about stimulating the provision of private rented housing. As a result, private sector tenancies created after 1988 are deemed to be assured tenancies (or assured shorthold tenancies), for which a market rent may be charged. In the case of housing associations, new tenancies are likewise required to be assured tenancies, with the slight difference that in the majority of cases 'affordable rents' are chargeable. The nature of the difference between market rents and affordable rents is discussed in Chapter 7.

Assured shorthold tenancies
Assured shorthold tenancies were introduced with the 1988 Housing Act, and differ from assured tenancies in that they have a fixed term, which must not be less than six months' duration. From the landlords' point of view they afford the maximum of flexibility in deciding the letting period.

Tenancies which continue to be protected under the Rent Acts
The 1988 Housing Act allows for the phasing in of assured tenancies where existing tenants are concerned. This means that only in cases where there is a change of tenancy or a change of landlord, can an assured tenancy be created. Existing protected tenants continue to be protected under the Rent Acts. This means that 'Fair Rents' continue to be assessed and charged in this sector, and tenants continue to enjoy a high degree of security of tenure. Fair Rents are discussed in detail in Chapter 7.

Returns on investment

In deciding whether or not to invest in rented housing landlords consider the potential rate of return on that investment. For a private landlord that return relates to the capacity of a given housing investment project to cover its costs of purchase, construction, management, and repairs, and still generate a financial yield or profit. For the social landlord, including housing associations, this yield is calculated in terms of the financial return but also the social benefits which will accrue from the investment. Let us consider the two sub-sectors in turn.

Private landlords and commercial returns
Behind a private landlord's decision to invest in rented housing is an assumption about the size of the financial yield which is anticipated. In the past, rent controls have been blamed for limiting the ability of landlords to generate surpluses, and this was widely believed to have acted as a disincentive to landlords considering investing in rented housing. The removal of rent controls under the 1988 Act is a direct response to this problem.

The contraction in the numbers of private sector tenancies is part of a general long-term decline, which has been punctuated by the imposition of rent restrictions in 1974, 1977 and 1980. Concern has been voiced by campaigning organisations and also by the Duke of Edinburgh's Inquiry into British Housing[4] about the effect of the growing shortage on the young and mobile in particular. As a result, taken within the context of the Government's fiscal incentives to owner occupation on the one hand, and its capital spending controls on local authority provision of housing on the other, the question of how to stimulate production by encouraging investment in private rented housing has become a significant policy issue.

To be attractive to investors, private sector housing must be able to compete favourably with other investments from the point of view of income generation and capital growth. Until now however, government incentives to private landlords to provide housing have concentrated on freeing up the landlord's yield, rather than on encouraging the initial capital investment. Landlords are not eligible to borrow money in the form of a mortgage to make their initial investment. They are thus excluded from the type of tax benefit attached to mortgage tax relief, and so borrowing is more expensive for the private landlord than for the owner occupier. For most investors therefore, the principal attraction of investment in housing is the prospect of the capital gains likely to accrue to them as a result of rising land and property values.

Most landlords treat their involvement in private rented housing as a long-term investment. In common with other investments however, within its term, there may be opportunities for short-term gain. If for example a landlord owns property in an area which becomes the subject of a major area improvement initiative, or which suddenly benefits from new developments in transportation or other external pressures affecting demand, that property may become particularly desirable, leading to 'windfall' capital returns. Starting from a point where equilibrium in the market for that particular type of rented housing is assumed to exist, this change in conditions will be expressed by a shortage in supply. If the landlord then wishes to maximise the returns on the property concerned, the rent could be increased to a figure which represents the present value of the future likely returns on the property, assessed in the light of the changing fortunes for the area within which the house is situated.

Market theory suggests that the excess profit or yield which the landlord makes through increasing market rents in accordance with the change in the market structure, will be of short-run significance only, as the market, now in disequilibrium, returns to equilibrium. The prospect of 'excess profit' will act as an incentive, attracting new landlords into the area concerned, and encouraging some existing landlords to put additional housing units onto the market. The result is that the temporary shortage will disappear, and supply may even increase beyond the point of equilibrium. The effect this will have on slowing present values will be one of levelling off market rents and moving towards long-term equilibrium.

In theory, therefore, the successful functioning of the self-regulating market depends upon the ability of landlords to be free to act upon opportunities for short-term yields. In this situation, rent controls have been taken to imply rent losses to landlords. A Government study of the private rented sector in 1982 found that a growing number of relets appear to avoid or evade rent control, and one third of landlords in a group which mainly let for financial reasons expected not to relet when units become vacant. This appears to account for the progressive withdrawal of many private landlords from private renting.

For most investors in private rented housing, their financial involvement amounts to a long-term commitment, and the returns on their investment are spread over a number of years. In view of the long-term nature of their investments, there is an argument that landlords ought to be entitled to expect a competitive rate of return which takes full account of that long-term commitment. A figure of 10% was quoted in a major DoE survey of the rented sector in 1981[5] as being a rate of return which landlords would find acceptable and thus maintain their interest in the sector. The same survey found however, that the rate of return to landlords on property with registered Fair Rents was 3–5%. Even despite the large potential capital gains to be made in some parts of the country upon sale of property, considered in relation to other forms of investment, housing had become a poor performer. As landlords withdrew from private renting, and the shortage of private rented housing became apparent, so the pressures for relaxing the rent regulation provisions of the Rent Acts understandably grew.

Housing associations and social returns
Whilst the primary concern of private sector landlords is gain in relation to the costs of acquiring and maintaining their investment, the housing association sector, in its role of providing social housing to complement the provision of local authorities, has concentrated on the social dividends associated with the financial costs of provision. Housing associations have their origins in the 'housing societies' of the 1950s and 60s, which were funded principally by covenants and donations. This uncertain source of funds was supplemented by a small government subsidy and capital loans from the building society movement. The opportunity for housing associations to organise as a movement and establish themselves as an important arm of housing provision came with the establishment of the Housing Corporation in 1964. The Housing Corporation was given powers to regulate and fund housing associations through the provision of loan capital, which enabled their activities to expand in a systematic way.

Several developments during the last 25 years have helped to define the current role and function of the Corporation, starting with its establishment in 1964, as a devolved arm of the then Ministry of Housing and Local Government, with responsibility for the developing area of 'cost-rent' housing activity in which housing associations were involved. With the 1972 Housing Finance Act and the 1974 Housing Act, the relationship of the Corporation to its housing association clientele was clarified and strengthened. Together these two acts of Parliament gave the Corporation a financial base and extended lending powers, as well as a number of responsibilities with regard to the supervision and monitoring of the housing associations wishing to benefit from the loans it was now in a position to offer. This was effected by means of a registration procedure. In addition to registering with the Housing Corporation, non-profit making associations must also register as such with the Registrar of Friendly Societies. The incentive effect of the increased funding available through the Housing Corporation for housing associations, has, since 1974, seen the mushrooming of housing association activity throughout Britain. At the beginning of 1988 there were over 2600 registered housing associations in operation.

An unknown number of associations exist which are not registered with the Corporation, and these include for example some charitable associations, almshouses, and tenant management co-operatives, as well as more recently established associations which are taking advantage of private funding or are involved in such work as development for sale or leasehold. None of these rely upon, nor are they eligible for Housing Corporation funding.

As socially responsible landlords, housing associations have a 'corporate image' which is enshrined in the activities of the Victorian philanthropic societies established by for example George Peabody and Octavia Hill. The 1977 Green Paper on Housing[6] put particular emphasis upon Local authorities developing existing working relationships with housing associations, to provide for those who could not otherwise obtain a decent home. Housing associations were seen as having a social rather than a commercial role to play in housing provision. Recently however, the issue of commercial yields has begun to surface in the discussion of the future role of housing associations.

Housing associations have until now concentrated upon providing housing at Fair Rents in line with their social purpose. Since 1974, the Government has funded the majority of this activity through the Housing Corporation's administration of capital grants and loans, and revenue grants. By the mid 1980s, the Government had become a major investor in the provision of housing by housing associations, as Table 2.4.1, below, demonstrates.

At the same time, as the government has moved towards practising a market ideology, so it has begun considering the possibility of diversifying housing association activities, and binding these more closely to the activities of the market. Along with the provisions of the 1988 Housing Act to abolish Fair Rents and replace them gradually with market rents, the Housing Corporation has been developing a role for private capital finance for housing association work. This has meant the development of a new funding framework, which has taken some housing associations outside the public sector. A new and different ethos of housing association provision is thus being created, one which departs from the welfare ideology, and which instead, with its reliance upon market rents, reflects the market ideology.

The following discussion looks in detail at the capital financing of the activities of the 'independent' rented sector, with private landlords and the housing association movement considered separately. We will then deal with the developing links between private sector interests and the work of housing associations.

Table 2.4.1 Housing Corporation investment, 1985–88 (£mn)

	1985/86	1986/87	1987/88
Government subsidy	745.7	735.3	808.4
Receipts (home ownership sales, right to buy sales, Grant Redemption Fund, etc)	112.9	144.7	139.9
Total investment	858.6	880.0	948.3

Source: Housing Corporation Annual Report 1987/88

Private sector landlords

Stemming the decline in private rented housing
In 1900, the private rented sector accounted for about 90% of accommodation; today the figure is less than 10%. In part this is explained by the growth of local authority involvement in rented housing, and the growth of owner occupation. Throughout this century, private investors have turned away from providing rented housing for low income households and towards a variety of less problematic investment outlets.

The problematic nature of private rented housing as an investment is attributable to a number of factors. Profitability in the private rented sector has declined. In the post-war period, emphasis has been on expanding home ownership, and this was helped by the availability of cheap land and building labour. Governments intervened by introducing legislation which held landlords accountable for public health requirements, and there was also legislation to protect the security of tenure of tenants. Furthermore, income from property let in the private sector was taxed more heavily than much other business income.

More recently, as has already been explained, rent controls, with us for most of the century, have also been cited as a reason for the decline of investment in the private rented sector. 'Fair Rents' registered by Rent Officers have been seen as failing to provide landlords with the necessary revenue for carrying out repairs, let alone realise a yield from their investment input. For many private landlords, the 1988 Housing Act was said to be an opportunity to charge realistic rents which will allow proper maintenance to take place.

With the burden of repairs in public rented housing assessed at £20bn, and in the belief that this would occupy the public purse for a long time to come, the Duke of Edinburgh's Inquiry into British Housing in 1985 reexamined the role of the private rented sector and the reasons for its decline. At the same time the Government's former Minister of Housing, William Waldegrave, expressed concerns over private rented housing:

> We must stem this decline by making the provision of rented homes a sufficiently attractive investment for the independent landlord[7].

As a result of these considerations, a number of schemes which envisage the participation of the private sector in housing provision were contained in the 1988 Housing Act. These include schemes for transferring local authority stock to Housing Action Trusts (HATs), and for the transfer of local authority and other public sector stock to landlords registered by the Housing Corporation. Both of these schemes are designed to take property out of the public sector and lever private finance into their upkeep.

Nonetheless, evidence from campaigning groups like Shelter, as well as from Lord Scarman during International Year of Shelter for the Homeless (IYSH), showed how appalling conditions at the poorer end of the market, for example in bed and breakfast accommodation, can be. Much investment in private rented housing is tied up with the needs of vulnerable, low-income households who are locked into that sector by virtue of their poverty. For such people, private rented housing is the only accommodation to which they can gain access. HATs and transfers of public sector stock to 'approved landlords' are unlikely to solve such problems of gaining access to housing. The dilemma for the private rented sector then revolves not only around the identity and motives of the investor and the scale of their investment, but also around the financial resources of the consumers and their lack of market power.

Incentives and the investment decision
The decision of private landlords to enter the private rented housing business is influenced by their assessment of its investment potential. That decision has important consequences for revenue income. The investment potential of individual projects will also be assessed in this way, and may, for example, influence landlords' decisions on which out of several possible projects to pursue. This might involve comparing revenue projections for, say, a project based on acquiring a site for redevelopment with another based on converting a large house into flats. Also fundamental to landlords' initial investment appraisals is the knowledge that their activities will be taxed on the basis of rents being classified as earnings on investment, rather than these earnings being classified as business income.

Unlike other commercial business operations, private rented housing does not benefit from the system that provides for capital allowances to be set against tax. Few people would be willing to sink funds into business capital without the incentive of tax exemptions or allowances on that investment.

The one short-lived exception to this state of affairs involved an attempt to introduce capital allowances for private landlords under the Finance Act of 1984. This concession was restricted to landlords who were providing assured tenancies in new build rented housing under the 1980 Housing Act, as mentioned above. Under these provisions, in the first year of trading, 75% of capital costs could be offset against tax. These provisions were short-lived and were abolished in 1986. The

Business Expansion Scheme (BES), referred to later in this chapter, is an attempt to restore them.

Investment appraisal and capital costs

The way in which landlords appraise their investment and calculate their return is also likely to influence the extent of their initial capital outlay, which in turn will have a direct influence on the nature of the accommodation to be provided.

If, for example, a private landlord is considering a redevelopment or a conversion, with the aim of providing houses for rent, the revenue link will inform such decisions as the number of dwellings to be created, the decoration and service standards in the dwellings, the quality of the materials used, the final rent levels, and so on. High standards will mean a high initial capital cost to the landlord; a larger number of units and higher rents will increase the likelihood that there will be sufficient annual revenue not only to service any capital loan repayments being made by the landlord, but also generate earnings on that investment.

The landlord's motivation: investment appraisal and yield

At the centre of a commercial investment appraisal is a calculation which compares future anticipated yields with present capital costs. The investor is concerned with the *opportunity* cost of their proposed investment. Simply put, this involves considering whether the project under consideration really is the best place for the investor's money capital or whether a *more satisfactory* return or yield might be acquired by putting the money into some other investment project. Such a calculation brings together the following considerations:

1. The cost of borrowing or committing money capital (i.e. the rate of interest);
2. The value put on future costs and services (i.e. the discount rate);
3. The anticipated yields over the life of the project;
4. The security of the investment and its potential for capital appreciation;
5. The ease with which the investment can be realised if liquid funds are needed in the future;
6. The cost and convenience of managing and servicing the investment;
7. The availability of investment incentives which have the effect of reducing the real cost of the investment.

With respect to rented housing, the anticipated yields are directly related to rent levels and from a commercial point of view freedom to set rents which reflect market factors is seen as important. In this way, it is argued that legislation which has the effect of controlling or regulating rents discourages landlords from entering the market and also discourages existing landlords from improving, repairing and maintaining their properties.

In recent years property investment in most areas has been seen to be relatively secure and to have a potential for capital value growth.

However, the exchange value of a dwelling is affected by the existence of any tenancy rights which might exist over the property. Such rights may also make the property more difficult to sell at short notice thereby inhibiting the landlord's ability to convert his or her property investment into liquid funds. In this way it is argued that legislation giving tenants security of tenure has had the effect of discouraging investment in private housing for rent. It is in response to this that the present Government has introduced assured tenancies and assured shorthold tenancies, which are specifically designed to limit the tenant's long-term interest in the property by restricting tenants' rights to security of tenure.

A further general disincentive to investment is that, in comparison with many other types of investment, rented property tends to be difficult and expensive to manage. Not only have the buildings to be maintained but also satisfactory landlord and tenant relationships have to be cultivated and maintained.

Capital incentives and the Business Expansion Scheme
The 1988 legislation is about expanding the territory of the private landlord. Nonetheless, as has been said, little encouragement is offered to private landlords in the way of capital incentives.

The 1988 Budget however, brought an announcement on the Business Expansion Scheme (BES), originally set up in 1983 to channel investment towards high risk business ventures involving new technology. The scheme was then extended to include individuals and companies willing to fund schemes for acquiring and building houses for rent. The key idea is that the tax concessions investors receive under the scheme help to lever investment into private rented housing.

The scheme works by offering opportunities to higher rate tax paying individuals to invest sums of up to £40,000 in new companies which conform to the scheme's criteria of eligibility, in this case companies involved in private rented housing. The investor in return receives tax relief on the sum invested and dividends from rental income.

Anyone financing company landlords under the BES will qualify for tax relief until the end of 1993. The housing can be purpose-built or related to existing properties, with a maximum threshold on the costs per dwelling of £125,000 in London, and £85,000 in the rest of the country.

In the first year of the scheme, some commentators have put the likely cost to the Government in tax lost through tax relief at £40mn. Private landlords operating through the Business Expansion Scheme will thus have an important financial advantage, in that they will effectively be capitalised through wider private sector investment, giving them a stronger position — initially anyway — in the market place in relation to non-BES capitalised companies. The BES provisions are intended to replace the earlier unsuccessful system of capital allowances to corporate landlords involved with letting new build housing under assured tenancies, referred to above. An important point about the BES provisions however is that they favour the short-term investment, and it remains to be seen whether housing, essentially a commodity of long-term significance, can satisfactorily be funded through this mechanism. In essence this questions the ability of BES capitalised companies to continue to attract investment after 1993, when the benefits of tax relief will end.

Building societies
Building societies also operate in the private sector. They received a direct message from Government to get involved in private rented housing in the form of the 1986 Building Societies Act. This established powers for societies to finance, develop, build and manage private rented housing projects. The changes had been long awaited by the Building Societies Association, but in reality, the response has been tentative.

Probably the most important scheme to be announced to date is the 'Quality Street' initiative. Set up by Nationwide/Anglia Building Society, who have invested £600mn in the company, it is involved in putting together projects for private rented housing in collaboration primarily with local authorities. It predicts that it will own and manage 40,000 rented homes around the country by 1992. The deals which it expects to put together with local authorities rely heavily on negotiated permutations of the barter approach.

However, success depends upon the degree to which rents can be held within affordable levels, and some building societies operating similar very much smaller scale initiatives believe that the Building Societies Act failed to provide financial incentives adequate to tackle the problem of making schemes viable. This question of viability is of particular importance in areas of the country where land values are high: the costs of land acquisition are carried through to pricing policy and so rent levels are as a result, high. Consequently, they consider government must act if societies are to become involved in providing rented housing at all.

Sources of finance
Until now, the majority of private landlords have not been developers other than in a fairly humble way, but rather acquirers of property for letting. The majority of private landlords are individuals, and small 'non-company' businesses. There are many individuals who let their property as a temporary measure as a matter of expediency while for example relocating or working abroad. At the upper end of the scale, there are also a number of corporate landlords who may be developers or companies whose investment portfolio includes residential property along with a variety of other interests. There remain two additional sources of finance available to landlords to help fund capital works to property.
1. *Public sector grants*   Under the 1974 and 1980 Housing Acts (as consolidated by the 1985 Housing Act), local authorities have been able to assist private landlords by providing renovation grants. The 1989 Local Government and Housing Act proposed a new system of grants. The grants systems are described in detail in the next chapter. At the time of writing, grants are awarded to landlords (or owner occupiers) for specific

purposes — for providing standard amenities, and for major repairs. In return, the landlord agrees contractually with the local authority that the dwelling will continue to be let.

2. *Private finance* Outside capital repair and improvement works, private landlords must fall back on their own resources or on the financial institutions for credit. Companies wishing to become involved in providing private rented housing now have the option of securing outside investment through the Business Expansion Scheme, as discussed above. In the case of building society lending, mortgages are not available on property which it is intended should be privately rented, and any borrower letting their property in this way is in breach of their mortgage agreement.

The main suppliers of credit are the banks, especially through business lending and development schemes. Building societies are also important providers of non-mortgage finance, and in addition, insurance companies are often involved in the provision of capital finance for corporate landlords engaged in urban development projects. Private landlords operating as companies may also use existing profits to underwrite a stock issue, raising the prerequisite finance for their undertaking on the stock market. In practice this mechanism is more associated with major property development activity, of which housing for rent (but more usually to buy) is provided as part of a wider commercial development.

The new private landlord

The reforms for housing in Britain provide for the registration of new 'social landlords' by the Housing Corporation, to provide and manage rented housing under assured tenancy arrangements. These approved 'social landlords' will operate in the private sector, and are expected to have a role to play in taking over the management of formerly local authority owned housing estates, under the provisions for voluntary transfers ('pick–a–landlord'). Housing associations are eligible to operate these schemes, and it seems that a few companies and building societies may also have an interest in working in this field. In general, the new social landlords are expected to be institutions rather than individuals or small landlords. At the same time, there are moves within the private sector to establish a service base for the 'new landlords', in the expectation that agents or 'factors', such as lawyers or estate agents will be required to manage clients' property interests.

The success of government strategy in attracting the interest of all of these bodies however is highly dependent upon the consumer issues which were identified earlier and which will be discussed further in Chapter 7; namely the levels of the market rents which the market will bear, bearing in mind that the structure of the demand for privately rented housing contains a large proportion of people who are either on very low incomes, or who rely entirely upon state benefits.

Capital finance and Housing associations

The structure and function of the Housing Corporation

The housing association movement is funded for the most part by a government quango, the Housing Corporation. The Housing Corporation has a national and a regional structure. In the first instance, there are three 'national' corporations; the Housing Corporation which covers England; Scottish Homes, formed in 1988 out of a merger between the Housing Corporation in Scotland and the Scottish Special Housing Association; and Housing for Wales, formed out of the Housing Corporation in Wales under the terms of the 1988 Housing Act. The term 'the Housing Corporation' thus now refers only to the English operation. By April 1989, all three corporations became independent of Government in that they became wholly responsible for the management of development programmes and for the entire administration of grant funding. The implications of such a change will become clear later in this section. The discussion here will be confined to the Housing Corporation as it operates in England, though most of the principles hold true for Housing for Wales.

The Housing Corporation's main function is to be responsible for developing the activities of the housing associations throughout England. In addition under the terms of the 1988 Housing Act, it provides advice to, and is responsible for the registration of landlords wishing to become involved in the management of stock transferred from public sector ownership, as well as advising tenants of public sector housing which might be the subject of a stock transfer.

The Corporation is accountable to a board of management and a chief executive, all of whom are appointed by the Secretary of State for the Environment, and to whom it also makes its annual report. Until recently, and in common with government agencies such as the former Manpower Services Commission, it submitted a 'Corporate Plan' annually to the DoE, which was intended to provide a strategy for future Corporation investments over a five-year planning period. In 1987/88, this system was suspended, in line with the Government's desire to encourage the Corporation to become more independent.

The Housing Corporation acts the role of 'banker to the housing association movement'. In this role it pursues the chief objectives of efficiency and value for money, with the expectation that the housing associations with which it is involved will exercise the same discipline in their financial affairs. This concern with value for money is expressed through the Corporation's funding practices, which stress the need to target funds towards identified housing needs and to use publicly provided funds to leverage private investment. Some of these practices will be discussed in detail shortly.

Though the Corporation is beginning to be joined by other institutions wishing to become involved in the funding of housing association activities, its role in relation to the development of the movement as a whole is particular and defined by statutory provisions designed

of capital grants to housing associations. The vast majority of associations continue to benefit from a HAG subsidy, though the nature of this capital grant itself is altered.

The main objectives of the new arrangements are:

(i) to provide a framework in which as many schemes as possible can take place on a mixed funding basis and so increase output in relation to the Corporation's public funding budget:

(ii) to simplify procedures and give associations more control over development decisions;

(iii) to increase 'cost consciousness' in associations, by placing tighter constraints on subsidy, and sharing financial risks between the Housing Corporation and associations themselves[9].

The main point to note about the new system is that HAG is no longer calculated after completion of an individual housing association project, on the principle that those capital costs which cannot be met by rental revenue will be picked up by the grant calculation. Instead, the level of HAG to which an association is entitled for a particular type of project, perhaps in a particular area, is agreed *in advance*, before work begins. Any cost overruns which occur while the project is on site and which exceed acceptable limits are the responsibility of the association; associations are thus required to manage costs effectively.

Another important change has been to fix the precise levels of HAG on an annual basis. This means that a housing association for example carrying out rehabilitation work in Bristol can establish, before it even submits projects for approval to the Corporation, what level of grant it is entitled to. In turn, when that grant level is fixed, factors relating to the geographical region, as well as factors relating to rehabilitation work are taken into account. The levels of grant themselves which are proposed for the first year of the new regime (1989/90) have been the cause of controversy. This is because they have been set at levels which are below the majority of 'traditional' HAG settlements. The key concern here is that as housing associations have to fund this increased proportion of their capital costs out of rental income, rent levels will be pushed up, and may become unaffordable for tenants on low incomes.

A final point is that some categories of housing association provision, in particular special needs housing, and more difficult rehabilitation projects, have in the past received HAG at 100% of the project cost. These so-called '100% Public Funding' schemes are intended to be phased out by the early 1990s. Grant levels have been high for these schemes because associations' anticipated rental incomes have been low. In order to reduce the proportions of public funding which are paid out in such cases, it is not only a matter of raising rents, now possible under the 1988 Housing Act for assured tenancies. Given that the tenants of much special needs housing may have no income other than that paid through state benefits, it is also a matter of adjusting benefits, including housing benefits, thus transferring the subsidy from the producer — the housing association, to the consumer — the tenant.

In sum then, *the* fundamental difference between HAG in its original form and HAG under the new system is that grant is paid 'up-front', at the start of development, rather than at the end of the development period, as has been the case until now. HAG under the new system is therefore calculated on the basis of *projected* development costs and not on *actual* development costs. Where development costs overrun the initial estimates, HAG remains fixed at the level previously agreed between the association and the Housing Corporation. The effect of this is to transfer the risk associated with the control of development costs to the housing association, where under the old system this risk was borne by the Housing Corporation.

It will take some years before the new system of capital finance for housing associations takes effect. For a period therefore, projects which were initiated by associations before the 1988 Act took effect will continue to be funded under the old system of 'traditional' HAG.

Table 2.4.2, below, gives details of the new fixed HAG rates for the year 1989/90, and demonstrates how these vary between regions (represented by the 'cost groups') and types of development work. All figures are for the percentage of actual development costs which are considered eligible for HAG.

The capitalisation of the Housing Corporation   The Housing Corporation thus acts as the vessel through which the subsidy of HAG is administered, and also lends money to housing associations in tandem with HAG. The Corporation's own capital income breaks down into subsidy and loans.

The non-returnable subsidy is awarded annually by the Treasury to the Housing Corporation, which in turn passes on these funds to housing associations in the form of HAG. This sum of money is voted expenditure; that is to say that Parliament votes annually on its level

Table 2.4.2 Housing for rent — provisional rates for HAG, 1989/90

Scheme type	Cost group						
	A	B	C	D	E	F	G
New build:							
— standard	81	79	75	74	70	67	63
— off-the-shelf	78	76	71	70	66	63	59
— works only & traditional schemes	75	73	68	67	63	60	57
Rehabilitation:							
— standard	87	84	82	81	79	79	78
— existing satisfactory	84	81	79	78	76	76	75
Sheltered:							
— Category I	83	80	77	76	72	70	67
— Category II	90	89	86	86	85	84	83

Source: *Housing Association Weekly*, 27th Jan. 1989

through the minor debates and acts of empowerment which follow on from the annual publication of the Government's Expenditure Plans in the spring (see Chapter 2).

As well as this annual Exchequer grant, the Corporation borrows funds from the National Loans Fund, a Treasury borrowing facility, to fund its lending activity. The Corporation in turn makes regular loan repayments to the Fund.

Public sector borrowing restrictions Whilst it is often felt within the housing association movement that associations could provide more housing, there have for some years now been financial limitations upon their doing so. One reason for this is that the Housing Corporation is restricted in the amount of money it has available annually to lend. A more important reason is that the money the Corporation borrows from the National Loans Funds counts as public sector borrowing. The present Government is committed to reducing public expenditure through restricting public sector borrowing and restoring financial incentives. Recently, this has been pursued through imposing limitations upon the Public Sector Borrowing Requirement.

Faced with these restrictions, though also with the prospect of its lending power being effectively extended, the Housing Corporation has been encouraged by the Government to persuade housing associations to seek private funding for some of their projects. An important incentive has been a modification to Treasury regulations which relaxes some of the PSBR accounting rules on mixed funding developments (private sector finance plus subsidy), so as to effectively take them outside the ambit of PSBR accounting. This has had the effect of removing borrowing controls on both housing associations and the Housing Corporation, giving a generous degree of freedom to borrow from private sector, at a time when local authority borrowing is subject to increasing controls.

Allocation of funds; Approved development programmes, programme agreements and tariff agreements

The Housing Corporation has a regional network which it uses as a framework for administering the lending activities which have just been referred to. It has firmly defined spending programmes and procedures for allocating its funds. The Corporation plans both its mixed funding and public funding programme expenditure through the use of spending plans known as 'Approved Development Programmes' (ADP) and Programme Agreements. In 1989, Programme Agreements are to operate in conjunction with 'Tariff Agreements'. Under this system, the Housing Corporation is expected to assess the suitability of individual associations to work under the discipline imposed by private finance. This assessment, based on the assets available to an association with which to cushion financial risks, determines the general conditions under which the association receives funding.

The national ADP refers to the annual programme of subsidy and loan funding agreed between the Corporation and the DoE. The amount of subsidy which the Corporation receives for reallocation to housing associations as HAG is fixed by the annual Public Expenditure White Papers and ensuing acts of parliament, with the amount it can lend to housing associations being fixed by Government imposed cash limits.

Within the ADP, as well as for the purpose of negotiating programme agreements with individual associations, there are two main spending categories, and a third special category which has been introduced recently.

1. Rent Housing   covers family housing, sheltered housing for the elderly, hostel and shared accommodation, as well as funding for major (capital) repairs and short-life projects. In the past, this category has been known as the Fair Rent programme. It is important to note also that from April 1989 HAG for capital repairs has been discontinued.

The Corporation controls expenditure on the rent programme through a system of spending controls based on *blocks* of expenditure, as follows:

Block 1: Committed Expenditure: This permits control of expenditure on projects which the Housing Corporation has already approved, and which are underway during the accounting year in question.

Block 2: New Tenders Approved: This controls spending on projects which, once tenders are approved, go on site during the accounting year.

Block 3: New Rent and Hostel Projects: This concerns any spending incurred on schemes which are approved for lending purposes by the Corporation during the year. In effect the overall costs of all individual projects are treated as Block 3 expenditure at some stage in their history.

2. Low Cost Home Ownership   covers a number of special initiatives which involve housing associations in selling property. Currently these include improvement for sale, leasehold schemes for the elderly, shared ownership, and home ownership for tenants of charitable housing associations.

Expenditure within this spending category of the ADP is controlled through loan approvals given during the accounting year. Low cost home ownership also provides the Corporation with a source of income once the housing provided is sold.

3. Flexible HAG   As has been said earlier, in 1987 the Corporation introduced this new programme of funding, which provided a reduced grant, known as 'Flexible HAG'. It was aimed at those associations prepared to develop projects under 'mixed funding' arrangements, but with a considerably reduced HAG contribution. The overall intention of the scheme was that public subsidy and private sector borrowing be combined to fund development work and that the majority of funding for such projects be drawn from the private sector.

Within the programme, three areas were targeted: the homeless, particularly in London; job movers; and 'Challenge Funding'. The Challenge Funding budget was aimed at general needs, and intended to introduce housing associations to the possibilities of mixed funding as a mechanism for funding project work. In the scheme's first year of operation, associations were required to find the remaining 70% of their project finance from the private sector. Many housing associations however, were put off by the risks that this level of private sector borrowing entailed and the effect that it would have on rent levels. The decision by the DoE to allow the Corporation to raise grant levels from 30% to 50% in 1988/89 responded to some of these concerns, allowing associations to get involved in mixed-funding schemes while still benefiting from substantial public subsidy.

The national ADP, whose structure has been outlined here, is composed of the development programmes or Programme Agreements of the entire housing association movement in England. A housing association's negotiated Programme Agreement thus amounts not only to a share of national strategy, but also a share of national public subsidy. The Programme Agreement represents the second level through which the Corporation allocates funds.

Programme Agreements are rolling programmes of development approved in principle by the Housing Corporation with individual housing associations, to which the Corporation agrees to commit a proportion its funds. This amounts to giving permission to go ahead with a particular scheme, subject to the projected costs of development. In the first instance the agreement commits the Corporation to lend to an individual association, and in the second, to meet the cost of the HAG to which the association is entitled. Prior to 1989, all associations had negotiated Programme Agreements with the Housing Corporation. From April 1989, these agreements fall into two broad categories, 'Tariff' and 'Non-tariff' agreements.

Tariff Agreements are aimed at associations carrying out mixed funding projects, and introduce a three year planning cycle, as well as allowing the 'pooling' of project development finance. Associations will contract to meet defined housing needs in stated areas through the production of specified numbers and types of dwellings. HAG will be paid at a fixed rate ('the tariff') per dwelling, on the basis of grant levels for mixed funding laid down annually by the Corporation. In theory, the tariff procedure will allow associations to plan their capital expenditure over a period, and will give them more independence and flexibility to programme activity. Given the financial risks associated both with the new system of HAG being paid in advance of the development period, and with the use of private sector finance, it is clear that only those associations which possess the necessary managerial and financial skills, and surpluses needed to provide a financial 'cushion', will be attracted by the new arrangements.

The Non-tariff Procedure, the other category of Programme Agreement, takes account of those associations which do not have very large development programmes, but still are able to move towards mixed funding. It is also designed to support those associations who still need to rely on high levels of public funding and who do not have easy access to private funds.

The General Needs Index

Once the Housing Corporation has received its loan finance and subsidy allocations for its budget year from government, it then goes about deciding how to allocate those funds across the country. For this, it uses a modified version of the DoE's General Needs Index to assess the need for investment in various areas of the country.

The DoE General Needs Index is based upon a nationwide analysis of a range of social, economic and environmental factors affecting the quality of life. The index attempts to map these factors, and rank geographical areas as a function of their various characteristics. Thereafter, Government uses the index as a basis for allocating public funds both to local authorities and other centrally funded agencies or projects.

The GNI system was first adopted by the Housing Corporation in 1983/84 and is used as a basis for allocating funds for Block 3 expenditure (New Rent and Hostel Programme), as described above. It is used both as a basis for allocating funds between Corporation regions, and also as a guide for the distribution of funds within regions and at local authority level.

In theory the GNI measures factors contributing to housing supply and demand in each local authority area. The Housing Corporation's modified version excludes two main factors: the demand for mortgages, and the number of dwellings in need of repairs grants. This is because these are seen as principally local authority rather than housing association concerns. It also gives a more important weighting to demand for specialised housing.

The GNI system of allocating funds has received a great deal of criticism over the past few years, much of which has argued that what goes into the GNI calculation is subjectively decided upon, and thus produces a rather arbitrary assessment of needs. The GNI, it has been argued, may give a reasonable assessment of needs at a given point in time; however, it cannot take account of the less quantifiable needs, such as hidden homelessness, which is not always accessible through local authority waiting lists, or the need to plan for needs caused by changes in Government policy, such as the recent planned closures of large institutions for the mentally handicapped[10]. Slavish adherence to GNI-linked principles of capital allocation may be sufficient to tackle general needs, but may nevertheless result in some very specific or localised needs being neglected. To tackle this problem, from time to time the Housing Corporation as a matter of policy targets specific needs and areas for investment. The GNI is due to be replaced with a new Housing Needs Index in the early 1990s.

Additional targeting

On top of the GNI determined spending programmes then, the Housing Corporation has also paid attention to specific housing issues. For example, from 1984, the Corporation targeted rural housing as an area of concern, forging links with the Development Commission, a Government funded agency concerned with rural issues, particularly employment. This led to the registration of rural housing associations for the first time. Similarly, with the shift of interest towards housing conditions in the inner city, and pressure for more effective area renewal, the Corporation in 1987 targeted a number of towns and cities, designated under the Inner Urban Areas Act and referred to as 'stress areas'. It is clear that the introduction of Tariff Agreements, referred to above, may provide a further means for directing activity towards certain geographical or specific needs areas.

Eligibility for funding and the control of investment
It has already been demonstrated how it is essential for a housing association to be registered with the Housing Corporation if it is to be eligible to apply for loan funding from that organisation at all. Beyond this basic criterion however, are further constraints on eligibility with which a registered association must conform if it is to secure public funding. It is possible to group these constraints into the following categories: constraints upon administration, constraints upon project development, and constraints upon management. In addition, housing associations must also account for the way in which their funds have been spent, and this is done through the preparation of annual accounts in the form laid down by the Corporation.

The effect of these constraints is not only to control eligibility for funding, but also to provide the Corporation with a framework through which they can safeguard their investment. Checks and balances allow the Corporation to take action in cases where it is necessary to protect the tenants or the funds of an association, its housing stock, or the general reputation of the housing association movement.

Checks on administration
In connection with its monitoring role, the Housing Corporation visits housing associations to look at working practices and administrative systems. These 'monitoring visits' do not amount to an audit in the narrow financial sense, but rather concern themselves with the way associations manage their affairs overall. During such visits, the monitoring team investigates the key areas of administration — management, finance and development. They also look at how the management committee works, to ascertain that it is in control of the affairs of the association.

Thereafter, a report, or *Monitoring Profile* is produced, with a list of any action required on the association's part. Such reports can deal with major items such as the handling of project finance, as well as specific items such as the quality of minute-taking or filing systems. In the year following the visit, evidence will be required that the listed items are receiving appropriate attention.

Monitoring is not explicitly linked to the loan allocations process. There are cases however where the Corporation may find that an association has failed to respond to difficulties which were pointed out while it was being monitored. In such cases, or where far more serious problems are reported to the Corporation, it may use its powers to become directly involved in aspects of the association's work, and may even make statutory appointments to the management committee. The result of this whole process can be that a housing association will not be considered eligible for loan finance until its internal problems have been resolved to the satisfaction of the Corporation.

Checks on development
The project development phase is also associated with certain controls. The development process itself follows a rigid pattern, with specific regulations administered by the Housing Corporation, which require associations to act in a given way throughout, from site acquisition, to appointing and paying an architect and other consultants, drawing up plans, pricing the project, inviting and accepting tenders, project monitoring, and so on. The Corporation goes some way towards controlling development practice by issuing the *Schemework Procedure Guide*, which associations are recommended to follow in their development work. Projected development costs are controlled through the publication of *Total Cost Indicators* (formerly known as Total Indicative Costs), designed to impose ceilings on an association's spending on a given project.

This systematic series of controls, which are all linked to the application for, approval of, and payment of monies for the purchase of the land, the paying of consultants' fees, stage payments to building contractors, monthly progress reports, monitoring of final accounts, and so on, have the net effect that they oblige the Corporation's client associations to accept this practice if they are to benefit, payment by payment, from the HAG and loan finance which the Corporation has agreed to put their way.

The Corporation pays for and further controls the administrative side of development practice through the setting of 'development and acquisition allowances'. These are sums of money which the association may claim on a per dwelling unit basis to help cover administration costs associated with acquisitions, project assembly work for both new build or rehabilitation projects, and any decanting or rehousing which is necessary to allow the project to proceed.

Checks on management
Finally, an allocation of capital funds carries with it constraints on the management of the completed project. It has been shown how the Corporation directs funds through the ADP system towards Rent Housing and Low Cost Home Ownership. The implications for management are very simple: a project funded under the Rent component of the ADP, once completed may not be sold as Low Cost Home Ownership or vice versa. The scheme must be managed in accordance with the source of funds.

Accounts
Housing associations must produce a series of annual accounts which conform to accounting practice laid down by the Housing Corporation[11]. The annual accounts are intended to give a picture of the affairs of

the housing association in full, and are submitted to the Housing Corporation and the Registrar of Friendly Societies within six months of the end of the financial year. The accounts must contain: a Balance Sheet, a Summary Income and Expenditure Account, a Statement of the Source and Application of Funds during the year, the Property Revenue Account, a General Income and Expenditure Account for housing related activities, and a General Income and Expenditure Account for non-housing activities.

The capital transactions of the association are contained within the first three of these accounts, and also in the General Income and Expenditure Account. The recommended form of accounts laid down by the Housing Corporation requires that the first three accounts be accessible to non-specialist readers, such as committee members or tenants, and they are as a result clear and easy to understand. Capital and revenue items appear together throughout the accounts.

All housing associations consuming loan funding also keep internal loan accounts for each development project. These accounts track the regular loan repayments to the Housing Corporation, and are verified regularly against statements provided by the Corporation on the amount of outstanding loan.

Local authority funding and housing associations
The Housing Corporation has been the main provider of capital funds to the housing association movement. However, in some parts of the country, local authorities have promoted housing association activity in their areas and helped to fund their activities.

Local authorities have two main powers under the 1957 Housing Act where the finance of housing association activity is concerned: they may give grant aid, and they may lend.

Since 1974, and the introduction of Housing Association Grant to subsidise housing association borrowing, local authorities have been able to lend to housing associations and with the approval of the DoE, apply HAG to the cost of repayments. The DoE has required that local authorities wishing to support housing association activity in this way have their intentions written into the authority's local housing strategy, and that any costs involved in supporting this strategy be included in the bid for its Housing Investment Programme (HIP) allocation. Thereafter, it has been customary for the DoE to scrutinise local authority sponsored applications for HAG, sometimes on an individual project basis.

Housing associations have thus been able to apply for HAG *either* to a given local authority *or* to the Housing Corporation, with the lodging of two applications 'on spec' not being permitted. Associations have however sometimes faced delays when applying for loan funding through a local authority which already has heavy demands on its budget. This has been a particular problem for those whose activity was formerly funded by the metropolitan boroughs, abolished in 1986. Though applications for funding were transferred to the local borough councils following abolition in 1986, local authority budgets at that time were not correspondingly adjusted.

Under the terms of the 1988 Housing Act, the Housing Corporation will be responsible for the administration of all HAG claims. This means that those local authorities who lend to housing associations will in future apply to the Housing Corporation for HAG, rather than to the DoE. This is expected to simplify the overall administration of HAG.

Housing associations and the private sector

Since 1986, the main innovation in housing association funding has been in the area of private funding. This is linked to the Government's concern that ways be found of reducing public borrowing and public expenditure (see Chapter 2).

This view is based on the premise that growth in the economy is attainable through providing incentives, in the form of tax breaks, which encourage 'wealth creators' to create wealth, without any need for direct government intervention in that process. Following on from that line of thought, the task for the Government is seen as one of how to direct wealth generated in the private sector into housing. Housing associations, because they have been funded primarily by public funds are in most people's minds associated with the public sector. The attempt to reroute private funds into housing associations suggests some redefinition of their place with respect to the public–private divide. The 1988 Housing Act also signals the importance of private funding, and the need to rethink rent levels and tenancy conditions to provide the necessary climate to attract private investment.

Mixed funding schemes

As has already been explained, in 1987, the Housing Corporation, under pressure from the Government began introducing 'mixed funding' experiments, which relied upon a level of HAG of up to 30% of the capital cost of the project, with the balance of finance being provided where possible in the form of a loan from the private sector.

The Government intends that a growing proportion of the activity of housing associations be funded through a mixture of grant and private finance, though there is an understanding that the transition will be a gradual one.

The consequences of the introduction of mixed finance particularly affect the future management of projects, and the rent levels set. In addition, mixed funding schemes are not eligible for Revenue Deficit Grant, nor are they liable for payment of Grant Redemption Fund. Revenue Deficit Grant and Grant Redemption Fund are discussed in detail in Chapter 7.

Under the new regime, two main forms of HAG presently operate: the first in conjunction with Housing Corporation lending can be referred to as 'fixed' HAG; the second, a reduced rate HAG, is awarded where a housing association borrows both from the Housing Corporation, but in addition borrows privately.

The key macro-economic reason for introducing the mixed funding experiment, is that money raised privately need not fall under public spending controls, and so is not counted against the Public Sector Borrowing Requirement, the economic tool used by government to control aggregate public sector borrowing (see Chapter 2). Before 1987, if public and private finance were combined in this way, all of the borrowing involved counted as public sector borrowing. A change to Treasury regulations in 1987 meant that the reduced 30% HAG counted as public expenditure, but that the borrowing from the private sector no longer constituted public sector borrowing for government accounting purposes.

One of the results of this relaxation is that it can be argued that the public funds allocated to the Corporation can effectively be redeployed to generate additional activity, with the overall net result that more housing can be provided, without increasing the level of public spending.

At the time when these experiments were launched, there was considerable concern that this might augur the demise of HAG in its original form, which was capable of funding up to around 85–95%, and even 100% of capital costs where an association's revenues are low. The average HAG level under the new regime is presently 75% of approved project costs.

Apart from the management consequences referred to earlier, the idea that development programmes can be doubled through the addition of private funds however, thereby providing twice as many homes for the same amount of public sector investment, is an attractive one. The first Mixed Funding experiment, the 30% formula tested in 1987, targeted three areas of activity — housing for the homeless mainly in London, shared accommodation for job movers, and a mainstream programme where the formula became known as 'challenge funding'. In 1988, 30% HAG became 'Flexible HAG', with the Corporation able to approve levels of grant of between 50 and 75% on any type of scheme which would formerly have received full HAG funding. In 1989, with 'Flexible HAG' now part of the mixed funding initiative, grant levels have crept a little higher, with the result that the grant levels proposed for 1989/90 for mixed funding schemes are now identical to those announced for fixed HAG, and outlined earlier in this chapter.

We shall look at some of the issues of private financing of housing association activity in turn.

Organisational arrangements
In May 1987, the Government demonstrated its commitment to expanding the mixed funding formula by persuading the Housing Corporation to proceed with the establishment of a financial vehicle which would be responsible for raising and distributing the private funds needed to make mixed funding schemes operational.

This organisation is constituted as a trust and known as The Housing Finance Corporation (THFC). The Housing Corporation, financial institutions, DoE and the NFHA are all represented on the board of the trust. It is run jointly by the Housing Corporation, CIPFA, and a private stockbroking firm, and works with support from the Private Finance Unit which is part of the Housing Corporation. The Private Finance Unit intends to provide the regular operational links with the housing association client body. The scheme thus has a fund-raising arm and a fund-distributing arm.

The calls made on this central fund-raising body, it has been suggested, are unlikely to follow an even geographical pattern, with proposals coming mainly from those associations which are large and have good knowledge of private finance mechanisms. Others suggest that those associations working in parts of the country which have suffered from economic stagnation and withdrawal of corporate investment will make the heaviest demands on this central body. At the time of writing however, a general picture has emerged of individual housing associations successfully raising private sector funds without the need for recourse to THFC.

Private sector finance options and conditions
Moving away from the main route towards mixed funding — relying on HAG combined with private finance gathered through the vehicle of The Housing Finance Corporation or alternatively through private institutions, there are other models of collaboration involving housing associations and private finance.

1. Building society collaboration   Building societies in the past have been traditionally associated with the owner occupied market, and housing associations have been traditionally concerned with the rented market. Consequently, building societies without expertise in housing management confined their involvement in the rented sector to the lending of money to housing associations. Since 1987, and the passing of the Building Societies Act, building societies have been looking increasingly towards the rented market. The new powers of the Building Societies Act include development powers and the power to make unsecured loans. This will increasingly lead to building societies fixing upon housing associations as their 'natural partners' in providing rented housing. It should be pointed out however that there is a possible conflict between the interests of building societies and housing associations here, encapsulated in a comment by the Chief Executive of Nationwide/Anglia Building Society:

> 'Societies have got to make money out of this [rented housing] — we are not charitable institutions'[12].

Housing association–building society collaboration of this kind is already occurring. Some housing associations have benefited from index-linked loans. This has highlighted the possible use of index-linked finance from building societies. This is a particularly attractive form of borrowing from the point of view of housing associations, as the cost of borrowing is low in the first instance. The advantage for the building society is that the loan holds its value as it is continually linked to current prices. Being index linked, the disadvantage to the borrower however, is that the loans are linked to the rate of inflation, and any rise in that rate is passed on to the borrower in the level of loan repayments. Inevitably this means that these costs are passed on to tenants when rent levels are assessed.

Building societies also lend to housing associations through deferred interest and other conventional lending schemes. Such schemes can provide for sinking funds conceived with the cost of future maintenance in mind, and may also lay down terms for regular rent reviews.

Three-way partnerships involving a housing association, a financial institution and a local authority are a further example of such collaboration. Perhaps the best example of this is that of the 'Sheffield Partnership', set up in 1987 under the auspices of the local authority, who provided the necessary guarantees, and with the involvement of UK Housing Trust, the Banque Nationale de Paris and the Nationwide Building Society. The Sheffield Partnership is currently tackling a phased programme of area renewal, aimed at providing over 2,000 homes at an initial cost of £70mn[13]. Local authorities have used barter deals to make such schemes work. Some of these arrangements, which for example allowed local authorities to exchange land for, say, nomination rights once the housing was provided, depended upon guarantees provided by the local authority, a practice which is no longer legal.

2. *Share capital*   North Housing Association has used the mechanism of the stock issue to secure private funding for a 4,000 unit development programme of houses to be built for some 23 local authorities across the north of England. The principle behind North's initiative was to use reserves which had been built up over the years on its older stock once loans were paid off, to lever private finance into the programme. The way that this worked in practice was that an annual input of £3mn over the first four years of the programme is used to underwrite a stock issue of £100mn on the Stock Exchange: the association is thus borrowing from those individuals and companies who invest in its stock. The participation of local authorities involved in the scheme is confined to their providing sites at no cost in return for nomination rights, once the developments are complete[14]. This is another example of a barter deal.

3. *Other examples*   Outside these models of collaboration, there have been additional experiments by some associations to raise funds through other private means. These have included schemes involving both the domestic and international money markets, from conventional borrowing from both British and foreign banks and financial institutions, to share deals involving the establishment of Business Expansion Scheme funded companies which are serviced by 'sister' housing associations, and even 'Eurobonds'.

Obstacles to obtaining private finance
CIPFA has identified a number of obstacles which must be overcome if housing associations are to be successful at raising private finance[15]:

1. housing associations only require relatively small parcels of money at any one time, rather than the very much larger sums normally raised in the private money markets;

2. most City institutions are wary of investing in residential property;

3. institutions are nervous about government interference in social projects which make them more risky investments;

4. housing associations find it difficult to assess the asset value of the properties they own as many have sitting tenants;

5. housing associations, because of their lack of experience in this area of finance, can face problems when it comes to reading the money markets and trying to assess whether rising inflation is likely to create problems for them;

6. most city institutions have little knowledge or experience of housing associations. Their image as small voluntary bodies doesn't inspire confidence among investors;

7. borrowing money for rented housing requires long-term loans of 40 – 50 years duration.

All of these factors seem to support the argument that one strategic vehicle, such as The Housing Finance Corporation, is best placed to negotiate, create confidence, and lever private funding towards housing. The willingness of the Housing Corporation to act as guarantor in relation to private sector housing association borrowing also emerges as a factor likely to have a crucial influence on the financial institutions' confidence in investing in housing association activity. In turn, if private sector borrowing expands as it is hoped to do, the question as to whether such guarantees can be kept outside the concerns of the PSBR will become important.

Implications of private funding for project development and management

Earlier we discussed the implications of private landlords' investment decisions for the management of their property interest. Housing associations, and in particular those choosing to opt for a proportion of private finance in order to swell their development programme, are affected by the same concerns. These include a wide range of development decisions relating to such matters as density, size of dwellings, number of floors, overall standards of design, and monitoring of costs in relation to cost limits. These decisions taken together constitute an association's individual development style, and all of them impact upon the way in which projects are assembled and run after they have been completed.

Management style   Since the Audit Commission reports[16], local authorities have become used to the view that the management of housing ought to be conducted in a 'businesslike' way. The voluntary sector image of the housing association movement, with a management style which relies on a certain degree of informality and face-to-face contact, has already been noted as a possible obstacle to raising private finance. This 'user-friendly' style of management, which is particularly associated with the charitable housing associations, has begun to give way to a more 'professional' approach to association work. For some, the abandonment of the 'caring landlord' approach may be seen as a disadvantage of the forthcoming financial regime; others however may feel that given the task being thrust towards housing associations, it is time that a more managerial approach be adopted.

Financial implications   Housing associations operating mixed funding schemes are to be awarded one single government subsidy in the form of an initial reduced HAG contribution, which is paid 'up-front' at the start of development. Thereafter, an association will be expected to recover all its outgoings from revenue.

Under mixed funding rules, where HAG is considered as a one-off payment, no further relationship with the Government is assumed, and so therefore as one would expect, there is no entitlement to RDG, nor any liability for GRF (see Chapter 7). As a result, the association must meet loan repayments from revenue, and cover the rest of its outgoings on the development and administration of the scheme, including the annual cost of establishing sinking funds to assist in meeting periodic costs of repairs and maintenance.

Return of the cost rent programme

Before 1974, the housing association movement's housing programme was referred to as the 'cost rent programme', reflecting the then lack of reliance upon public funding. If under mixed funding arrangements, associations are required to recover the full extent of their outgoings from rental revenue, the cost rent programme can be said to have been revived. As we have said, the revenue issues will be discussed in more detail later; however one point can be emphasised at this stage. Until 1988, it was a condition that housing associations in receipt of HAG register rents as Fair Rents. Since the early 1980s at least there has been discussion over the levels of Fair Rents set by Rent Officers and the basis upon which these have been arrived at. It is a basic point that Fair Rent levels would have been insufficient to meet the costs of borrowing from the private sector. Market rents, introduced in 1989 to the housing association sector, are a necessary part of the framework to make mixed funding projects viable.

Conclusion

The twin agendas of the market ideology and the welfare ideology may be found in the motives of the private landlord and the housing association sectors respectively. Mixed funding experiments mean the introduction of the market ideology into the housing association sector. What nonetheless will continue to distinguish the housing association movement from the private landlord sector is that their new programme is likely to continue to be non-profit making in the commercial sense.

Despite the shift in emphasis towards cost rent projects brought about by the introduction of more private sector finance, there will nevertheless still be a need for associations to provide accommodation which can clearly be categorised as 'welfare housing'. Such schemes, which are likely to include most special needs housing, will probably continue to receive substantial capital subsidies from government. This is because these projects are unlikely to attract the private investor, perhaps as a result of their geographical location or the financial circumstances of their tenants, many of whom rely upon state benefits. Consequently, they will be viewed as high risk investments by the private sector, because they will not offer the prospect of a secure return to the investor.

Finally, we would point out that the nature of the demand for private housing is such that the new 'market rents' which are necessary to meet the costs of servicing private sector borrowing by housing associations as well as by private landlords, are likely to be unaffordable for many people. This raises the issue of the central role of housing benefit in meeting the income support claims of the poorest in society. The Government has made several statements on this:

> "The housing benefit system will give adequate assistance to people who cannot afford such rents"[17].

The success of the new regime hangs upon this commitment to provide adequate assistance to tenants through housing benefit, a commitment which implies a move towards subsidising the consumer rather than the producer of housing.

Notes

1   *Housing — the Government's Proposals*, Cm. 214, September 1987.
2   1974 Rent Act and the 1977 Rent Act; in addition the 1980 Housing Act introduced regulated tenancies and made them subject to Fair Rents.
3   The 1988 Act however ensures that all *existing* tenancies established under the terms of the Rent Acts retain their security of tenure.
4   *Inquiry into British Housing*, chaired by HRH The Duke of Edinburgh, NFHA, 1985.
5   House of Commons Environment Committee: *The Private Rented Sector*, HMSO, 1982. For more detail on this subject see Whitehead, Christine M.E. & Kleinman, Mark, *Private Rented Housing in the 1980s and 1990s*, Dept. of Land Economy, University of Cambridge Occasional Paper no. 17, 1986.
6   Department of Environment: *Housing Policy, a consultative document*, Cm 6851, HMSO, 1977.
7   William Waldegrave addressing the Institute of Housing, July 1987; text of the speech published in *Housing*, July 1987, p 32.
8   As set out in the 1974 Housing Act; modified by the 1980 Housing Act and summarised in the consolidating 1985 Housing Associations Act.
9   Housing Corporation, 'The Way Ahead – the Corporation View', (briefing Paper on the new grant framework for scheme procedures

for housing in England) in *Housing Association Weekly*, 7 October 1988, pp 8–10.

10   C. Holmes, 'If you value local judgements, beware the GNI' in *Voluntary Housing*, vol 33, no 1, January/February 1984, p 33 (adapted).

11   See update, 'The new financial regime for housing associations', in *Housing Association Weekly*, 16 December 1988.

12   Tim Melville-Ross, Chief Executive, Nationwide/Anglia Building Society, quoted in *Voluntary Housing*, December 1986, p 16.

13   *Housing Association Weekly*, 21 August 1987, p 3 (adapted).

14   *Housing Association Weekly*, 8 May 1987, p 1 (adapted).

15   Listed by Rachel Terry, CIPFA Services at NFHA *Public Finance Foundation Seminar*, 22 May 1987, and summarised in *Housing Association Weekly*, 29 May 1987, p 5.

16   Audit Commission, *Managing the Crisis in Council Housing*, HMSO, 1986; Audit Commission, *Managing Council Housing Maintenance*, HMSO, 1986.

17   William Waldegrave addressing the Institute of Housing, July 1987; text of speech published in *Housing*, July 1987, p 33.

Chapter 5
Capital expenditure on local authority housing services

Introduction

The finance of the local authority housing service has, for many years, been inextricably linked to the financing of all the other services they provide. Impending legislation seeks to weaken and perhaps eventually end these links but for the moment the relationship is still sufficiently close to justify an explanation of housing finance within the general context of local authority finance.

This chapter describes the mechanisms by which local authorities raise money to pay for their production, or capital, spending. In housing terms this means raising money to pay for the provision of new housing and for the cost of improving existing housing. Capital spending also has an impact on the running, or revenue, costs of the local authority. For example, new council houses will need to be repaired and maintained for perhaps 60 years or more after they have been built and this means that, in the local authority context, it is not easy to describe capital and revenue finance as though they were independent of each other. Some sources of finance are only available for capital purposes but most can be used for either capital or revenue purposes. For example, local taxation is generally raised to pay for the current running costs of a local authority yet in some circumstances it can be used to pay for production expenditure. The impact of the production of new housing on the running costs of a local authority and the mechanisms for raising the money to meet those costs will be dealt with mainly in Chapter 8.

Local authorities are subject to financial controls by the Government. These may take the form of direct controls, such as an instruction only to spend a given sum on a particular service, or the less direct control applied by giving grants and hoping that the local authority dependency on such grants will encourage spending behaviour in line with government plans. The targets set and signals given to local government come primarily from the Government's series of PESC White Papers, and this system has been described fully in Chapter 2. Chapters 5 and 8 are concerned with how these control totals are devolved to individual local authorities rather than the policy that directs how much spending power enters the system.

This book is written at a time when the Government, having introduced new controls on local authorities in 1979/80, is overhauling many of the systems. Some of the new controls and policies have already been approved by Parliament, others are still at the discussion stage. The current systems will be described and compared with their proposed replacements.

The management of housing services in local authorities

An introduction
The state has always been responsible for defending the realm and the provision of justice. During the eighteenth and nineteenth centuries it gradually extended its influence into a wider range of domestic affairs including poor law relief, law and order, working conditions, public health, education and housing. In order for the government to secure effective intervention in these areas there was a growing dependence on the evolving structure of local government. Local authority provision was seen to have the advantage of allowing decisions to be taken in the light of local knowledge and these decisions tested by local accountability. Broadly speaking the intervention has taken two forms: firstly, the detailed and strategic planning for local needs including land use planning, and secondly, direct involvement in the provision of certain services. The provision of the housing service emerged at the end of the First World War as part of the welfare agenda of the then Liberal Government.

There are 450 local authorities in England and Wales. At present these are responsible for delivering several major public services at a local level including education, personal social services, leisure services, rented housing, local planning and transportation, and the fire and police services outside London. In some areas the full range of local authority services and functions are provided by a single authority, such as a London borough council or metropolitan district council. Outside of the London Boroughs and metropolitan districts the services and functions are split between two tiers of authority; namely county councils and non-metropolitan district councils. The power to provide a service can be given by Act of Parliament or by instruction from the government department responsible for the national planning of the service. Such powers are usually given to a particular class of local authorities, so that, for example, county councils are responsible for providing education and non-metropolitan districts for providing housing. The mix of services is subject to change. From time to time Parliament imposes new duties on local authorities ranging from the responsibility to provide police and education services in the nineteenth century to the more recently imposed duties to provide accommodation for the homeless and administer the Housing Benefit scheme. Parliament can also take away from local authorities the responsibility for providing services if the government considers that other organisations will provide the service more effectively. Services that local authorities have provided in the past, but no longer have the power to provide, include the administration of the prison service and the supply of gas, electricity and water.

The government also, from time to time, has radically reformed the structure of local government, the last major restructuring taking place in 1974 when the number of local authorities in the United Kingdom was reduced from over 1,500 to a mere 522.

General functions and management of a Local Authority

A Council is elected by people eligible to vote and living in the local authority area and its function is to promote the welfare of its local population within the framework of policy decisions taken at a national level. Broad strategic policies are set by the political programmes of the elected members. The day to day administration of these policies is carried out by the paid officers who, as professionals with continuity of service, are also responsible for advising their political masters on technical matters including the legality of any proposed actions. In order to pay for the services provided the Council has the power to levy a local tax.

How the work of Local Authorities is organised

Local authorities are organised into departments, each of which normally has a Chief Officer responsible for its activities and for implementing the Council's policy for that department. Some departments are responsible for running a service or group of services. In addition the main professional services will also be centralised into departments, for example the financial services of the authority will be provided by the Finance Department, engineering services by the Engineer's Department and legal services by the Clerk's Department. The Chief Officers will meet regularly as a team to discuss matters that cross departmental boundaries. Most authorities appoint a Chief Executive responsible for chairing these meetings and ensuring that the decisions taken are for the general good of the local authority and not just to the advantage of one service department.

The Council of the authority meets regularly in full session but most of its work is done in smaller groups called committees. The committee structure is likely to be similar to the departmental structure in that there will be a Finance Committee dealing with financial matters on an authority wide basis working alongside committees appointed to consider the needs of each major service. These committees will be made up of members of the Council but may also include some non-voting co-opted members with special interest in the service, e.g. teachers sitting on the Education Committee. Any matters requiring decisions from the Council are put before the appropriate committee by the responsible officers. Recommendations made by each committee will be referred to the full Council where the implications of such recommendations for the authority as a whole will be considered. If the Council accepts a recommendation then the officers will be instructed to implement it.

Local authority 'funds'

If a decision of the Council has financial implications, either for collecting money or spending it, the officers must advise the elected members whether funds are available for that purpose. Local authorities operate 'fund' accounting which matches money collected from one group of clients with the spending on services to them.

The following simple example (Figure 2.5.1) of an organisation using fund accounts illustrates the advantages to the organisation of using such analysis and the control implications inherent in the system.

Example. An organisation is responsible for providing services to three groups of clients. The services are provided annually, with the customers paying at the beginning of the year and no surcharge during the year. The income and expenditure for the year is:

	£
Income	1,000
less Expenditure	970
Surplus of income over expenditure	30

Figure 2.5.1

This account shows how the organisation as a whole has performed during the year, it collected sufficient cash from clients at the beginning of the year to pay for the services it gave them during the year and to generate a small surplus. If for political or legal reasons the organisation wanted each group of clients to pay for its own services it could set up fund accounts, and analyse the financial transactions to show whether this objective was being achieved. It could also allow some subsidisation between groups if it wished. Such a scheme could operate to the following rules:

1. Three funds are to be set up — 'Group A Fund', 'Group B Fund' and 'Group C Fund'.
2. Money received from clients from Group A, Group B and Group C is to be placed in 'Group A Fund', 'Group B Fund' and 'Group C Fund' respectively.

3. The cost of services provided to clients from each group will be paid for from the funds for that group.
4. Any surplus at the end of the year on 'Group A Fund' can be used to meet end of year deficits on 'Group B Fund' and vice versa, but 'Group C Fund' must be self supporting.
5. Any end of year deficit that cannot be met by subsidy must be recouped from next year's customers.
6. End of year surpluses can be used to reduce the charges for next year's customers.

Diagram 2.5.1 shows how such a division of the entity into funds could work.

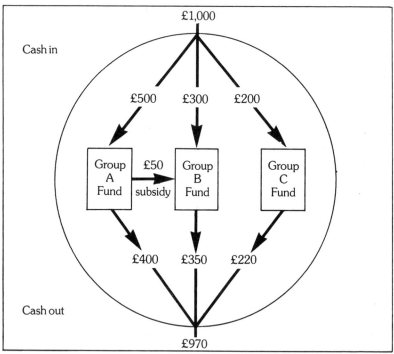

Diagram 2.5.1. Three funds within an organisation

By recording the financial transactions in funds the organisation can see that the clients in Group A (see Figure 2.5.2) are paying not only their own costs but also one seventh of the cost of the services for Group B clients. The Group C clients have not paid the full cost of this year's service and will have to pay higher prices next year so that the organisation can recoup the 'loss'.

It may seem inconsistent with the aim that each group should pay its way, that Group C clients received the full service in the year despite not

Group A Fund	£	£
Income		500
less Expenditure		
on Group A services	400	
subsidy for Group B	50	
	——	450
Surplus to reduce next year's charges		50

Group B Fund		
Income		300
Subsidy from Group A Fund		50
		——
		350
less Expenditure		350
		——
		—

Group C Fund		
Income		200
less Expenditure		220
		——
Deficit to be charged to next year's customers		(20)

Figure 2.5.2 Summary accounts for the three funds for the year

paying for its share of the service. However the organisation as a whole received sufficient cash to pay for the service and, in accounting terms, 'Group C Fund' borrowed the shortfall from the cash surplus of 'Group A Fund' and will have to pay back the loan from higher charges to be made to Group C clients in future. If the organisation as a whole had insufficient cash income to pay for the service provided it could borrow the money required to meet the shortfall from an outside source.

The extra information that these fund accounts give can be useful not only to the organisation giving the service but also to any organisation interested in controlling the use to which the service organisation puts its income.

The Government requires local authorities to keep fund accounts so that it can monitor the extent to which the incomes collected by the authorities from different client groups are used to subsidise each other. In the local authority housing context the Government is interested in the extent to which those who pay local taxes subsidise council house tenants and vice versa. Local taxes are paid into a 'General Fund' and are used generally to pay for the provision of services to local taxpayers as a whole. Council house rents are paid into a 'Housing Revenue' fund and are used firstly to pay for the provision of council houses. Any payments into the 'Housing Revenue Account' from the

'General Fund', or vice versa, must be clearly shown in the two fund accounts.

Housing authorities

Of the 450 local authorities in England and Wales, 403 have primary responsibility for the provision of housing services. These are the 33 London Boroughs, the 333 non-metropolitan districts, the 36 metropolitan districts and the Isles of Scilly. These are the 'Housing Authorities'. In addition, the 47 County Councils have reserve powers to help the districts in their area with housing matters if the need arises.

Although housing authorities have to work within a common legal and technical framework there are considerable variations amongst them. Some housing authorities will serve rural areas with a relatively small stock of well maintained houses, others will serve inner-city areas with a much larger number of houses, many in poor condition. For a non-metropolitan district council the housing service may be the most important it administers, while for a unitary authority it is matched in importance by the education service. The representative and democratic nature of local government means that, except where duties are shared, local authorities can act independently of each other.

Duties and powers of a housing authority

Housing authorities have a duty to ensure accommodation is available for certain homeless people and the power to provide accommodation for others. In order to fulfil their obligations local authorities have the power to build new homes for sale or rent, buy and renovate existing properties or help individuals or groups to buy, build or renovate homes. While the Council has a general responsibility to ensure that its residents have homes fit to live in, it does not have to provide these homes.

The authority is currently required to 'consider housing conditions in their district and the needs of the district with respect to the provision of further housing accommodation' and to this end 'shall cause an inspection of their district to be made from time to time with a view to determining what action to take in the performance of their functions' of repair, area improvement, slum clearance and houses in multiple occupation. Thus, the council is required to take an interest in all housing in its area regardless of tenure-base.

The 1987 White Paper *Housing; The Government's proposals* (Cm. 214) declared that the Government

> 'will encourage local authorities to change and develop their housing role. Provision of housing by local authorities as landlords should gradually be diminished, and alternative forms of tenure and tenant choice should increase ... Local authorities should increasingly see themselves as enablers, who ensure that everyone in their area is adequately housed; but not necessarily by them.'

How much needs to be spent on the production of housing

Any organisation wishing to plan for the future must start by defining its objectives and establishing its priorities. The objectives of a local authority will already have been broadly defined by government legislation but within those general objectives there are still many policy decisions to be made in order to transform those objectives into an operating plan. The officers and members responsible for administering the housing service will be responsible for providing an operating plan to reach its housing objectives, taking care not to exceed the powers given to the local authority by the Government.

Assessing local needs

Local authority housing production should be related to the housing needs of the area. In order to assess the current need to provide new housing in a district the Housing Officer could look at the 'housing waiting list', which lists the names of the people who have applied for rented accommodation from the council. Currently, there are about 1.3mn households on council waiting lists. The council will sometimes use a 'points system' to differentiate between applicants. Those that the council regards as having priority because they are disadvantaged will be given a higher points rating. If there is a considerable waiting list people with a low priority rating may be discouraged from applying for council accommodation. The reliability of this list as an indicator of demand will depend on how many households in need are placed on it and how well it is maintained. Even if it is updated at regular intervals it may still include the names of people who have found alternative permanent accommodation or left the area without informing the authority.

The authority will also need to consider the state of the accommodation currently offered. Is it of the right size and standard to meet the current needs of its residents? For example, the current housing legislation requires housing authorities to give priority to the needs of the aged and disabled, groups of people who may require special types of accommodation. The extent to which the authority is currently providing the right sort of accommodation might be reflected in the 'housing transfer list' of tenants asking to be transferred to more suitable accommodation. As a guide to policy, this list will probably be subject to the same limitations as the waiting list and, in addition, it will give no indication of the suitability of non-council housing.

The council may also be concerned by the extent of overcrowding in houses in its area and the need to renovate substandard homes. The extent of the problem should become apparent when the council inspects the district to assess this need.

A combination of these and other factors will show the extent to which the authority meets current needs. However provision of housing has long term implications. When a local authority builds a house it acquires an asset with a potential life of 60 years or more. It is only sensible to build the house in such a way that it can satisfy the expectations of the next generation of tenants and thus avoid the need for costly adaptations at a future date.

Future needs may be generated by changes in the size and structure of the population. These changes can sometimes bring surprising results. For example, between 1961 and 1981 the population of Bristol fell by 7.9%, but at the same time the number of households requiring accommodation rose by 9.0%. This paradox is explained by the trend towards smaller households, young parent families moving out of the city into the countryside at the same time that young single adults were moving into the city to live near their work. Future needs may also develop out of changing expectations of the quality of life. For example, inside toilets and running water, once considered to be luxuries, are now part of the standard amenities offered by local authorities.

Responding to the needs
Once the authority has assessed the need to provide for new or improved housing it must then decide to what extent it will match this need and how. The authority has the power, if it wishes and so long as sufficient resources are available, to provide all the housing needed. On the other hand, it may decide to encourage other parties to provide some, or all, of the accommodation. The extent to which a council decides that its residents require council rather than private sector housing will to some extent be a partly political decision.

The housing plan

Increased municipalisation
If the authority wishes to respond to the needs of its residents by increasing the stock of council houses available for rent it has the power to build new homes or to make new homes out of buildings not currently considered fit for human habitation. It may also repair and improve existing council stock. If the council wishes, it may carry out minor works to council houses as part of its works programme or it may agree to allow the tenant to arrange for the work to be carried out. For example, in the case of tenants' grants schemes operated by some authorities, individual tenants agree a schedule of work with the local authority. The work is then carried out by approved contractors under the supervision of the tenant, with the final cost being met by the authority.

However any marked increase in municipalisation would be contrary to declared Government policy: most authorities are more likely to seek to encourage private sector participation.

Increased private sector involvement
Increased private sector involvement in housing in a local authority area can be achieved in two ways: either local authority-built houses can

be sold to private sector buyers or the local authority can encourage the private sector to build or improve property by giving loans and/or grants in approved cases.

The sale of council-built houses can be at the discretion of the authority. For example if the authority decides that new buildings are required then it can build them for resale and, if it wishes, keep a financial interest in the houses by selling them under a shared ownership deal (see Chapter 3) whereby it sells, say 90%, of the interest in the house to the buyer and retains the remaining 10% in council ownership.

Local authorities also sell houses built for rent. They have had the 'right to sell' council houses built for rent since 1925 but theses sales were at the discretion of the authority. The Housing Act 1980 gave council house tenants the 'right to buy' the properties they rented, if they could afford to do so. This took the initiative away from the Council which no longer had a choice as to whether to sell.

The Housing Act 1988 seeks to extend privatisation by giving tenants the 'right to choose' a private sector landlord. If a suitable prospective landlord approaches a local authority and offers to buy council houses at the legally prescribed price, and a majority of those tenants voting in a ballot agree to the transfer, the local authority must sell to the bidder. The Act also seeks to introduce Housing Action Trusts (HATs). Boards of government appointees are given the power and funding to take over specified council estates if the majority of tenants agree to the procedure, improve the housing stock, and when their work is complete disband the HAT and sell the properties to the tenants, the private sector or back to the local authority. Since the legislation came before Parliament a small number of local authorities have announced their intention to sell off their council stock to private sector landlords as soon as possible. The financial implications of the privatisation of council housing will be dealt with in a later section of this chapter under the sub-heading 'Proceeds of the sale of assets'.

If the authority does not wish to be involved in the building of new houses it can encourage others to do the job by offering grants and loans for building purposes. The authority has the power to lend money to individuals and housing associations to pay for house construction. It can provide land, services, and materials at appropriate prices to self-build groups and lend them equipment and money. It can also help private sector builders by ensuring, through planning permission, that sufficient land is available for building.

Partnership projects where the local authority combines with a private sector organisation to provide housing are encouraged by the Government. Two main types of partnership scheme are popular:

— *Building under licence* allows the local authority to keep owner-ship of the land until the end of a scheme in which the developer occupies the site and carries out an agreed programme of work. When the houses are sold the local authority receives payment for the land. Often, in such partnerships the local authority has an exclusive marketing period during which the houses are sold to specific categories of buyers, sometimes at a discount.

— *Conditional land sales* are schemes where the local authority sells the site to the developer who then carries out an agreed programme of work.

Existing buildings that have the potential to be turned into effective housing accommodation will include housing currently unfit for human habitation. The authority may encourage others to do the necessary work. For example 'homesteading' involves the local authority in making a conditional sale of a house in need of substantial repairs or improvement to an individual. The sale carries with it the promise of grant aid to carry out these repairs and the purchaser in turn must carry them out to the satisfaction of the local authority. If the building is privately owned the authority has the power to lend money for its conversion to housing use.

The authority may also be concerned to improve the existing housing stock, whether council or private. If the houses are in private ownership the council can help, or in extreme cases force, the owner to make improvements or repairs. In the first case the initiative comes from the householder when they apply for grant assistance, in the second case the local authority has the power to initiate works through the issue of statutory 'notices'.

Initiatives from householders
The 'old' system
Help available in the 1980s Householder Initiatives: Grant Assistance

— *Intermediate grants* were mandatory grants paid to owners of houses (normally built before 1961) which lacked one or more of the standard amenities such as baths or a hot water supply, for a period of a year or more. The grant was also available to a disabled occupant in cases where the disability meant that a standard amenity had become inaccessible. The grant was made up of two elements, firstly a sum towards the provision of each of the standard amenities and secondly a sum for repairs needed to put the property in order.

— *Improvement grants* were designed to assist owners or tenants of pre-1961 houses, with a rateable value of less than £225 (£400 in London), to improve their accommodation up to a standard which would provide satisfactory housing for at least thirty years. They were discretionary except in the case of disabled occupants and owners of housing located in a Housing Action Area (see later). The discretion lay with the local authority which sought to ensure that such monies were used towards the improvement of dwellings to modern standards or to provide additional homes through conversions. The grants could cover a wide range of work of improvement or repair, but works of improvement must be the major element.

— *Repairs grants* were designed to help pay for substantial structural repairs on pre-1919 dwellings.

— Authorities had the power to make *special grants*. These were principally concerned with the provision of standard amenities and means of fire escape for dwellings in multiple occupation. These grants were discretionary except where the local authority issued a 'works notice' (see below) requiring the landlord to carry out specified modifications to the property.

— Home insulation grants were available in areas where the local authority had received government funding to operate a 'home insulation scheme'. Such schemes were designed and run on a basis determined by the authority subject to the Secretary of State's approval.

The 'new' system

The 1987 White Paper *Housing: The Government's Proposals* points to the Government's intentions to reform and simplify the grant system. The intention is to target grants towards people who need them, to encourage better take-up of grant, and to stimulate private investment. The Government will introduce a revised form of mandatory grant which will be available to bring property up to a new standard of fitness. Above this standard grant assistance will be at the discretion of local authorities. Grant entitlement will be determined by a simple test of household resources, taking account of the cost of the work that is needed and the householder's ability to finance such work from income and savings. It is expected that grants will continue to be available for the benefit of disabled people and elderly people will be helped with minor repairs and when they need to move in with relatives.

The Local Government and Housing Act 1989 proposes that the new grant system would allow local authorities to make *renovation grants* and *common parts grants* towards the cost of works required for the improvement or repair of dwellings and the common parts of buildings containing one or more flats, and for the provision of dwellings by the conversion of a house or other building. Owners of properties and tenants required by their tenancy agreement to carry out the relevant work may apply for grants as long as their property has been provided, by construction or conversion, for at least ten years, or some other period determined by the Secretary of State. An applicant must also provide a certificate stating that the dwelling will be the main dwelling for him or a member of his family for the next twelve months or, if he is a landlord, that the dwelling will be rented for the next twelve months. The basic grants offered will be equal to the cost of work done plus any eligible expenses but, as the new grants are to be means tested using criteria to be set by the Treasury, any grant payable to applicants may be less than the cost of the work to be done. If the proposed work is to be done to bring the dwelling to a state fit for human habitation then the basic grant will be mandatory but local authorities will also have the power to offer discretionary grants for works which go beyond those that will make the house fit for human habitation if the purpose of the work is to:

— put the dwelling in reasonable repair, or

- to provide the dwelling by conversion, or
- to provide adequate thermal insulation, or
- to provide adequate facilities for space heating, or
- to provide adequate internal arrangements.

The Secretary of State will be given the power to limit the amount of grant payable either by prescribing a maximum amount or by formula.

In certain cases, for example if the owner of a house renovated using a renovation grant sells the house within a year of the relevant work being completed, successful applicants may be required to repay any grants given to them.

The Secretary of State and the Treasury will decide what contribution will be made towards these grants from government funds and will have the power to prescribe a general rate or different rates for classes of authority, individual authorities and particular areas.

In addition to the two main forms of grant, grant is also available, subject to detailed regulations, for minor works, works to Houses in Multiple Occupation, and the cost of group repair schemes.

Grants to 'right to buy' owners
Since 1984 owners who acquired their properties under the 'right to buy' provisions may be entitled to financial assistance in respect of certain designated types of houses and flats which have been shown to have defects resulting from design failure. Normally owners are eligible for assistance where the defects became apparent after the purchase of the property. This form of reinstatement grant will normally cover 90% of approved expenditure subject to an expenditure limit. The authority has the discretion to give 100% grants in cases of hardship. Usually the occupier will be required to arrange for the repairs to be carried out. If the house cannot be reinstated at a reasonable cost the local authority can buy the property back from the owner. In such cases the authority must offer 95% of the defect-free value of the property and a secure council tenancy for the dispossessed household. The repurchase may involve the owner repaying part of the discount obtained under the 'right to buy' provisions if the repurchase takes place within 3 years of the purchase.

Local authority initiatives
Statutory Notices. These are issued to owners or landlords whose property lacks certain basic amenities. The improvement order requires its recipient to install specified amenities within an identified period. It is possible to appeal against such a notice. Such a notice contains the local authority's estimate of the cost of the works required to bring the dwelling up to 'full standard'

  Repair notices. These are issued to persons having control of houses declared 'unfit for human habitation' but capable of being made fit at reasonable expense. The local authority has power to enter any premises they have reason to believe may fall into this category. The repair order requires the owner or landlord to make specified repairs within a specified time. As with Improvement Notices, appeals are allowed. If a repair notice is issued and the owner does not obey its instructions, the council can carry out the work and require payment from the owner, if necessary by allowing payment by instalments with a mortgage on the property.

Works Notices. These are issued to owners of houses in multiple occupation in order to bring about works which are necessary as a result of 'neglect of management'. For example, a notice might be issued to provide additional and necessary lavatory or kitchen facilities.

Area approaches

The 'old' system

The Council could decide to identify a whole area as being in need of special treatment.

Area improvement. Where an authority could demonstrate that an identified area could be shown to be worthy of improvement they could declare either a General Improvement Area (GIA) or a Housing Action Area (HAA). Once the authority had achieved its objectives in improving the area the HAA or GIA was disbanded.

An authority could designate as a General Improvement Area any primarily residential area where it considered that the living conditions could be effectively enhanced by using the system of improvement grants. If a house was located in a GIA this would entitle the owner to a higher rate of improvement grant in the manner explained above. GIAs were more concerned with the improvement of the general local environment than with housing improvement as such.

An authority could designate as a Housing Action Area (HAA) any primarily residential area if it considered that living conditions were unsatisfactory and that they could be improved effectively in a period of five years. The authority had, in addition to its general powers to provide housing, the power to spend money on environmental works and to use compulsory notices coupled with enhanced entitlement to grants (see above). It also had additional compulsory purchase powers and could develop the land acquired for housing purposes or sell it to a housing association for such purposes.

The 1987 White Paper indicated that GIAs and HAAs would be replaced by a single form of statutory renewal area. Within such areas local authorities would be encouraged to develop a wider mix of renovation and selective redevelopment.

The 'new' system

The Local Government and Housing Act proposes that local authorities will lose the power to declare HAAs and GIAs and any existing HAAs and GIAs will cease. Local authorities will acquire the power to declare 'renewal areas' where they are satisfied that living conditions in a district consisting primarily of housing accommodation are unsatisfactory and that these conditions can best be addressed on an area basis. The Secretary of State is to be given powers to set conditions for the declaration of a renewal area, for example the minimum number of dwellings in the area and the lowest acceptable proportion of privately owned dwellings.

The objectives of the housing authority in a renewal area are to be:

— the improvement or repair of the premises, either by the authority or by a person to whom they intend to dispose of the premises;

— the proper and effective management and use of the housing accommodation; and

— the well-being of the persons for the time residing in the area.

To attain these objectives the authority will be given the power of compulsory purchase, subject to the approval of the Secretary of State, and the power to carry out work on land it owns and assist in works carried out on land it does not own by providing grants, loans and guarantees, doing the work itself or by providing materials for carrying out the work. The authority may also agree to hand over any or all of its functions under these powers to a housing association.

The Secretary of State, with the consent of the Treasury, will decide the extent of central government grant aid to renewal areas. The local authority may ask, and be given, more than the usual grants in special cases.

Area redevelopment. If a group of houses is considered 'unfit for human habitation' the Council can designate the area occupied by the houses as a slum clearance area, buy all the properties either by negotiation or compulsory purchase, demolish the buildings and redevelop or sell the site. This may require the rehousing of dispossessed tenants. If the Council decides to redevelop the site for housing purposes it is likely that some of the dispossessed tenants will have to be rehoused outside the area.

In addition to the powers below local authorities also have powers to lend money for the purpose of converting another building into a house, altering, enlarging, or improving a house, or for the purpose of facilitating the repayment of an amount outstanding on a previous loan made for any of those purposes. A loan may be made in addition to any grant assistance given by the authority in respect of the same house.

Capital finance budgeting

Capital finance budgeting is about turning a general policy into a specific plan. Once the authority has decided what housing is required and how it intends to ensure it is provided it can start preparing detailed programmes of work to be done. Decisions will have been made about the extent of grants and loans to the private sector and the changes to be made to the council's own housing stock. As indicated in Chapter 1 the finance that is used to add quantity or quality to the stock is classified as 'capital'. In other words, capital finance is the money needed to meet the production costs of the housing service. In the following discussion it is assumed that the terms production costs and capital costs are interchangeable.

The authority will have to consider the timescale of the plan, deciding whether it is happy to plan on an annual basis or to develop a comprehensive forward plan reflecting the policy decisions taken. The major disadvantage of planning on an annual basis is that many capital projects take longer than one year to complete. After approval in principle by the Council major construction schemes will require architectural and engineering design work to be done before the contract goes out to tender and the selected contractor can start the building work. If a local authority wishes to organise its affairs effectively it must take a long term view of planning, and prepare a capital programme looking at least three to four years into the future. This plan should be revised annually into a rolling programme.

In creating a housing plan the Council must consider the resources available to it over the planning timescale. The purpose of matching the basic housing plan to the resources available is to produce a realistic assessment of what can be achieved. New construction or building works will require materials, labour and, unless already owned, land. The scarcity of one of these may be a limiting factor in the authority's plan. For example, in recent years local authorities have built fewer houses and as the building industry has contracted, regional shortages of skilled carpenters and other craftsmen have emerged. Even if the authority had access to as much of the other resources as it needed, the shortage of skilled craftsmen could mean that it has to proceed more slowly with building work than it would otherwise do.

In order to buy the goods and services needed to realise the technical plan the local authority must arrange for sufficient money to be available to pay for the work done. The plan can be financed from money assembled from various sources. These sources include current income from ratepayers and rentpayers, grants from the Government, borrowing, leasing or from the sale proceeds of council houses. There are limits on how much cash can come from each source, some of these limits being determined by council policy and some from the systems used by the Government to control public expenditure.

For finance purposes the funds available to pay for capital expenditure can be analysed into two categories, payment from monies collected in the same year as the asset is acquired and funding that delays payment for the asset, usually spreading the cost over several years.

Paying for assets from current fund income
The following three methods of raising the money required to pay for capital expenditure all use current funds and their impact on the finances of the local authority is equivalent to the impact on an individual of paying for goods or services from salary or wages. Two of the methods mentioned, current income from ratepayers and rentpayers and capital receipts, may also use balances of monies that have not been spent in previous years, the equivalent for an individual of paying for an asset from personal savings.

— *Current income from ratepayers and rentpayers.* The current income of a local authority comes from charges for services (including the rent for council houses), local taxes raised and government grants intended to pay for revenue expenditure. The bulk of current income is used to meet revenue, rather than capital costs. However, if current income were large enough, it could be used to pay for all production expenditure as well. In practice, few, if any, local authorities could afford to do so as the level of local taxation required would be politically unacceptable to most Councils. Any expenses, whether capital or revenue, charged to a fund must be matched by income to that fund. This means that if the cost of providing a council house was to be met from the housing revenue fund then at least part of the cost of the house would be met from extra charges to the rentpayers in that year.

— *Proceeds of the sale of council houses.* If the local authority sells a capital asset it can use the proceeds, the 'capital receipts', for capital purposes only: that is, for the financing of new capital expenditure and the repayment of loans raised to pay for existing capital assets. Money raised in this way is put in a capital receipts fund and used only to pay for capital expenditure.

The major source of capital receipts for a housing authority is the sale of council houses built for rent. The selling price is based on a market valuation which, in the event of a dispute, can be referred to the District Valuer who is an employee of the Inland Revenue. Discounts on the agreed valuation of properties are offered to tenants as an inducement to take up their right to buy. Currently, tenants are offered discounts on the agreed valuation on houses of 40% after 2 years and a further 1% per year up to a maximum of 60%. More generous discounts are offered on flats, 44% after two years and 2% per year up to a maximum of 70%, in recognition of the reluctance of tenants to buy properties that carry future commitments to unknown levels of management charges and the problems of shared repair and maintenance. There are two limits on the size of the discount available, both set by the Secretary of State. The discount must not exceed a specified amount (this limit as amended in 1987 is £35,000) and the price paid to the council must be at least the 'cost-floor' of the building, an amount based on the cost of provision and improvement of the building.

This chapter is concerned with the impact of such sales on Housing Authorities, the impact on the tenant is considered in Chapter 6. The amount of the sale proceeds that a local authority receives each year from the sale of council houses under the 'right to buy' will depend on how the buyers raise the money to pay for the properties. The selling price of a property will be the agreed valuation less any discount, and a cash buyer would hand over this amount to the local authority in the year of sale. But few buyers will be in a position to pay over such a large amount of cash, most will have to borrow all or part of the money. Buyers can apply for mortgages to financial institutions such as banks and building societies specialising in such loans. If they are given a mortgage by such an institution then the local authority will be paid the full selling price at the time of purchase, any deposit coming from the buyer and the balance from the financial institution. A buyer who cannot pay in cash for the property and cannot raise a loan from a financial institution, perhaps because of age, is entitled to a 100% mortgage from the local authority. This loan will be repaid over a maximum of 25 years at a nationally prescribed rate of interest which matches or exceeds the rate charged by the building societies. The amount owed to the local authority will be paid over the period of the repayment of the loan and could be as little as 4% of the selling price per year. The total of capital receipts from the sale of council houses in any year will be made up of the selling price of properties sold to tenants who paid in full, either from their own funds or with the help of a financial institution, and any repayments of mortgages given by the local authorities to buyers past and present. The interest paid by the borrowers is not classified as a capital receipt but as current income and can, therefore, be used to finance either capital or revenue spending.

The cash flow from houses leaving the authority under the 'right to choose' legislation and the creation of HATs is less certain. The authority should receive the agreed value of the properties in full but there is still some uncertainty about selling prices.

— *Government grants to pay for capital expenditure.* There were no capital grants from the Government to help pay for capital expenditure on housing assets, such grants as were available being made to help pay revenue expenses including debt repayment. *The 'new' system.* The Local Authority and Housing Act 1989 proposes that the Secretary of State should offer grant aid towards the cost incurred by local authorities in making grants to the private sector and the cost of Renewal Areas by making a 'contribution' towards these costs. Such contributions would be capital grants and the money received from the Government would have to be placed in a capital grants fund and used to pay for expenditure supported by the grant.

Delaying payment for capital assets

Individuals who wish to obtain the benefit of the use of assets they cannot afford to pay for from their salaries or savings may choose to acquire the asset by borrowing money to pay for it and paying back the loan from current income. Other methods of acquiring the use of the asset without having to pay the market price on acquisition include renting and leasing. These alternative methods are also used by local authorities to fund capital expenditure.

i   *Borrowing.* Local authorities borrow money to pay for houses for much the same reasons that individuals take out mortgages for house purchase; if a house built by a local authority was paid for from current income then its capital cost would be paid for by that year's tenants. If however, as is invariably the case, a loan is raised for that purpose then there will be an annual payment to the lender which will have to be paid for from rents collected from successive years' tenants. The advantages claimed from borrowing are that it not only allows the authority to acquire assets it could not afford to acquire from current income but also allows the cost of those assets to be charged to a succession of tenants over the period in which they enjoy use of the house.

It is generally considered good financial practice to borrow long term to pay for an asset with short term life but imprudent to borrow long term to pay for current spending. In line with this general philosophy local authorities are allowed to borrow long term money to pay for the acquisition of capital assets but any borrowing for current revenue spending must be repaid within a year. Local authorities are also required to keep borrowing to pay for revenue spending to less than 20% of total borrowing. Local authority debt is secured on the revenues of the authority not, as is common in the private sector, on its assets. This is considered appropriate because the authority cannot carry out its statutory function if the assets are seized by creditors.

Just under 60% of all capital expenditure is financed from borrowing either by internal borrowing, when a fund that needs to borrow money will borrow from a fund with a temporary surplus, or by borrowing from external lenders. The most important source of external borrowing is the

Public Works Loans Board (PWLB). The PWLB is financed by loans raised by the Government and lends money to local authorities at rates prescribed by the Treasury. Because the Government can raise money more cheaply than any other organisation, the PWLB can offer loans to local authorities at below market rates. Each local authority is given a quota based on percentages of its capital programme and existing debt and can borrow this cheap money up to the amount of its quota. The PWLB also acts as a lender of last resort, but if it does so demands a higher rate of interest. PWLB loans are available with terms of three to sixty years and at fixed or variable interest.

The authority may also issue various types of borrowing instrument all offering the lender the repayment of the loan with some form of monetary income, usually the payment of interest. The main difference between instruments issued is the extent to which they are negotiable, that is tradeable in a money market, and whether the instrument is recorded in a register maintained by the authority. 'Stock' and 'bonds' issued by local authorities can both be used to borrow the long term funds required and 'bills' can be issued to borrow money on a short term basis.

An authority wishing to borrow a sum of money in excess of £3m could make a *stock issue* to be redeemed several years after the money is raised. The timing and terms of stock issues have to be approved by the Bank of England. The issue will be made through the Stock Exchange and the stock will be fully negotiable, this means that an investor buying local authority stock has access to a national market if he wants to sell it. The local authority will keep a register of owners, changing this each time stock is sold to ensure that the twice a year interest payments are sent to the current owner. The advantages of a stock issue are that it allows the authority to borrow a large sum of money in one operation, and that the stock will not have to be redeemed for many years. The disadvantages are that it is expensive to raise — issue through the Stock Exchange means employing stockbrokers and others familiar with such transactions — and expensive to administer, with changes to stockholders registers required each time stock changes hands.

Local authorities also issue *bonds*. Bonds are relatively simple, transferable in whole or in part and issued in two forms, 'local' and 'negotiable'. Local bonds are issued across the counter by local authority staff and, although they can be transferred to another owner, have limited appeal to investors in other areas. Negotiable bonds, which are registered and transferable in London, have greater appeal because of the ready market available in the capital. The timing and terms of issue of negotiable bonds are approved by the Bank of England, which requires that the minimum issue is £0.25mn. Bonds have most of the advantages of stock without the expense. Bonds can be variable or fixed interest with repayment after a period of at least one year. As with stock issue, local authorities issuing bonds will keep a register of owners.

Bills differ from stock and bonds in that they do not attract interest, but are issued at a discount. Names of owners do not have to be entered on a register, the local authority merely repays its debt to the person who presents the bill on settlement date. The payment of a higher price on settlement than the original 'cost' of the bill replaces interest. The timing and issue of bills has to be approved by the Bank of England and they are traded on the Stock Exchange. Bills are short term instruments and must be repaid within twelve months.

In borrowing money the local authority has to consider the financial consequences of the varying maturity dates of the loans being taken up. When interest rates are perceived as being historically high it may be considered good practice to borrow short rather than commit the local authority to paying high long term interest rates even when the market rate has fallen. However it can also be considered undesirable to have too much short term debt all repayable in the very near future. Local authorities adhere to a *voluntary code of practice* that requires them to order their long term borrowing so that in any financial year the average period to maturity of new loans taken out is not less than 7 years.

The Consolidated Loans Fund. If a fund such as the General Fund needs extra cash it will try to borrow money from another fund that is temporarily in surplus, failing that it will have to borrow from outside the authority. Many local authorities operate a special fund, the 'Conslidated Loans Fund' (CLF) to deal with borrowing transactions. The managers of this fund are responsible for ensuring that sufficient money is available to pay for the expenditure of the authority. All surpluses on funds are deemed to be loaned to the CLF and can be lent to any fund needing more money. When a lending fund needs the money back to meet the purpose for which it was collected the CLF will ensure the money is available either from other internal sources or by borrowing from an external source. In this way the local authority ensures that it only borrows externally when internal funds are inadequate for its purposes. Diagram 2.5.2 illustrates the relationship between the CLF and the funds used to finance capital expenditure.

For at least the last 150 years the Government has sought to control the level of capital spending and/or borrowing of local authorities and the controls it imposes on these are the major constraint on the level of borrowing by local authorities. These constraints are discussed in detail below.

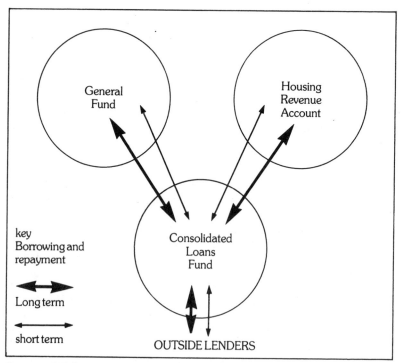

Diagram 2.5.2. Financing capital expenditure

ii   *Leasing.* It is not necessary to buy an asset to enjoy the use of it. In some cases it may even be cheaper not to buy it. This can be the case with leasing, where the leasing company may enjoy tax concessions not available to local authorities. Leasing, which accounts for about 5% of local authority capital expenditure, is mostly used to acquire the use of plant and vehicles, but it can be used to acquire the use of other assets.

For accounting purposes leases are defined as either 'operating leases' or 'finance leases'. An authority entering into a finance lease would not acquire ownership of an asset but would acquire substantially all the risks and rewards of owning the asset. In these cases the authority would usually acquire an almost lifetime use of the asset and pay 90% or more of the cost of the asset over the leasing period. Any lease not classified as a finance lease would be classified as an operational lease. As a general rule the use of assets acquired under finance leases are treated as capital assets, while the use acquired under operating leases are treated as revenue expenditure.

Financial constraints on capital spending

Having considered the funds available to pay for capital schemes and the constraints, if any, placed on them the next stage is to look at controls on the level of spending.

The 'old' system

The system lately operated was introduced in the Local Government Planning and Land Act of 1980 and subsequently amended. The major control on the capital expenditure of a local authority was the amount of money central government allowed it to spend on 'prescribed expenditure'.

Capital expenditure can be defined as expenditure on assets that give value for more than one year. Most of the production expenditure listed above will come into that category but not all of it increases the value of assets owned by the authority. For example the loans and grants to the private sector improve private sector assets not local authority assets. It is, therefore, important for the Government to carefully define the expenditure it wishes to be treated as capital and that is suitable for long term financing. Under the old system this was identified as 'prescribed expenditure'.

For housing purposes 'prescribed expenditure' was all spending on the acquisition of land and buildings, vehicles and equipment (only items costing £6,000 or more) and the construction of buildings. If repairs and maintenance of buildings were financed from loan it was 'prescribed expenditure', but if financed from current funds it was non-prescribed. Any loans or grants made for capital purposes were also 'prescribed'. Almost all 'prescribed expenditure' was capital, the major exception being 'repairs and maintenance' which is usually considered to be a current or revenue expense but for the purposes of capital control it could be considered as either capital or revenue, the distinction here being made, not according to the nature of the asset, but according to the way it was financed.

Under the 'old' system each local authority was given an annual 'Capital Expenditure Allocation' which allowed the authority to spend that amount on prescribed capital expenditure and to raise new long term loans to that amount during the financial year in which the allocation is given. The capital expenditure allocation could be supplemented by transfers from other similar allocations given it in past and future years and by transfers from other local authorities. The power to spend could be increased by using a proportion of capital receipts earned before the end of the financial year in which the allocation was made.

Capital Expenditure Allocations (CEA)
The Government determined how much money local government should be allowed to borrow for capital purposes, this was included in the PESC White Papers (see Chapter 2). In arriving at this figure it decided what level of capital spending it wished to see for the following year and the extent to which authorities as a whole were likely to supplement the CEA by the use of capital receipts. In England the amount available was then divided into six blocks, one of these blocks was for housing prescribed expenditure (the Housing Investment Programme, see below), the others were for education, personal social services, transport, urban aid and other services. Local authorities were asked to bid for the blocks allocated to the services they were responsible for. The Government then divided each block between the local authorities bidding for it, doing this on its interpretation of the need to spend for each authority without reference to its ability to pay for capital expenditure from internal funds. The CEA given to each local authority was the sum of its shares of these blocks.

How much a local authority could spend in a year on prescribed expenditure
The Government was concerned that local authorities collectively should not borrow more than the national total of CEAs and was, therefore, prepared to allow virement or swopping of CEAs. Virement between blocks given to an authority was permitted. For example, if the authority wished to use part of its education block to finance housing expenditure that would be acceptable. Virement between local authorities was also allowed. If for instance a County Council wished to encourage a district in its area to provide some housing services it could give part of its allocation to that district. Virement between years was also allowed, subject to the total enhancement being limited to a figure equal to 10% of the year's CEA. This meant that the amount a local authority was allowed to spend on capital schemes under this system in 1988/89 could be made up as Figure 2.5.3. The enhanced CEA also represents the maximum the authority was allowed to borrow for capital purposes.

The authority was to be allowed to increase its power to spend, but not to borrow, by a proportion of its net capital receipts. In England,

	£mn
CEA for 1988/89	11.4
+	
Any unused CEA 1987/88	0.6
+	
Some of the 1989/90 CEA	0.5
+	
CEA transferred from another Local Authority	1.9
Enhanced CEA	14.4

Figure 2.5.3

in 1988/89, the proportion of net capital receipts on the sale of council houses allowable to increase the power to spend was 20% and for other asset sales 30%. For example, if an authority sold council houses during the year for which it received £1mn in capital receipts it could spend an extra £200,000 (£1mn × 20%) on 'prescribed expenditure' over and above its enhanced CEA. The remaining £800,000 could be carried forward to be part of the 'net capital receipts' of 1989/99, when if the proportion remained the same, the receipt could be used to justify additional 'prescribed expenditure' of £160,000 (£800,000 × 20%). In any year the net capital receipts will be the total of capital receipts for the year plus any capital receipts from previous years not already used to justify 'prescribed expenditure'. The system of allowing only a proportion of capital receipts to be used to increase spending power was called 'cascading'. The amount the authority will be allowed to spend on 'prescribed expenditure' in a year will be the enhanced CEA plus the allowed proportion of net capital receipts.

If in the example Figure 2.5.3 used above the same authority had housing net capital receipts of £4mn and other net capital receipts of £1mn see Figure 2.5.4.

	£mn
Power to spend and borrow	
Enhanced CEA	14.4
Increased power to spend	
20% × housing net capital receipts (20% of £4mn)	0.8
30% × other net capital receipts (30% of £1mn)	0.3
Enhanced power to spend	15.5

Figure 2.5.4

This authority would have the power during the year to spend £15.5mn on 'prescribed expenditure' and the power to borrow up to £14.4mn to finance such expenditure.

How much could be spent on housing?

In theory almost all or almost none of this enhanced CEA could be made available for housing prescribed expenditure. With a few exceptions all spending powers could be vired between blocks. In practice it was likely that the authority would use the blocks for the purposes intended. This had a certain administrative simplicity and left the responsibility for sharing the allocation to the Government.

Housing Investment Programmes in England

The system for allocating permission to spend to housing authorities is known as the Housing Investment Programme (HIP). Each year housing authorities submit to the Department of the Environment a housing strategy and investment programme consisting of five elements.

- i.   The Housing Strategy Statement which sets out the authority's perception of the housing requirements of its area and the policies and priorities that lie behind its choice of programme.
- ii. The Housing Needs Appraisal Statement (Form HIP 1) a numerical statement providing a statistical picture of the authority's public and private housing stock together with information about households in need, relets of council houses and loans for the purchase of private sector houses.
- iii. The Financial Statement (Form HIP 2) which quantifies the housing strategy in both financial and statistical terms. It is a four year plan, covering the previous, current and next two years.

     The bid for the housing block is made on Forms HIP 2 and HIP 3. HIP 2 contains bids for expenditure on new house building, slum clearance, renovation of council houses, acquisition of existing dwellings for housing use, private sector renovation and investment grants, lending to private individuals and housing associations and payments for defective buildings.
- iv. The Low Cost Home Ownership Statement (Form HIP 3) bids for permission to spend on low cost home ownership schemes (these are discussed in Chapter 3).
- v.   The Long Term Vacant Dwellings Statement (Form HIP 4) provides details on houses which have been vacant for more than one year.

The local authorities are asked to prepare these documents in May to bid for capital expenditure allocations for the following year. The allocation for the next financial year, based on the information in the documents, is given to them in November/December, three months before the financial year starts. Authorities may receive additional capital allocations during the financial year.

Criticism of the 'old' system

The 'old' system had few supporters. Local authorities disliked it because they considered that the degree of control of their capital expenditure undermined their ability to determine local policy according to the wishes of the local electorate and their ability to fund such policies. The Government disliked it because it did not force local authorities to conform to the national plans for capital expenditure. In August 1988 the Department of the Environment issued *Local Government in England and Wales, Capital Expenditure and Finance — a Consultation Paper* in which the Ministry proposed a new system of control for capital expenditure to come into effect from the beginning of the financial year 1990/91. In the Consultation Paper the Government set out its reasons for wanting to change the system. It gave four major reasons for wishing to change the current system.

i.   *Failure to control spending.* The 1980 system had failed to bring about net capital expenditure consistent with the Government's public expenditure plans. For example in 1986/87, according to the Consultation paper, the Government wanted net capital expenditure of £2,369mn and local government spent £2,698mn, which represents an overspend on the Government's target of 14%. The equivalent figure for the year before had been, from the Government's point of view, even worse with a perceived overspend of 52%. The discrepancies arose because the Government consistently underestimated the success of the 'right to buy' policy and the extent to which this allowed local authorities to enhance their CEAs.

ii. *Failure to match CEA to need.* The system brought about a distribution of capital spending power that did not match the need for expenditure. Housing authorities with few problems and a stock of desirable houses to sell to tenants with well-paid jobs will sell more houses than an authority with less desirable property let to poorer tenants. Yet the HIP allocations to authorities take no account of their ability to pay for capital expenditure out of capital receipts and assume that authorities at each end of the scale are equally dependent on loan finance. In 1986 the Audit Commission estimated that 35% of HIP allocations went to housing authorities with relatively few problems and that almost £800mn in borrowing approval was given to authorities that should be able to deal with their local housing problems without additional long term borrowing.

iii. *Loopholes.* The legislation governing the 1980 system did not prevent local authorities from undertaking capital expenditure above the levels prescribed. Local authorities wishing to spend more than they were allowed to expended considerable time and energy concocting leasing, barter and other schemes in order to evade the restrictions imposed by the Government. Loopholes in the law were exploited and then plugged as the Government introduced new regulations to try to impose its will on local government. Provisions in the 1988 Local Government Finance Act closed the most widely exploited barter and leasing loopholes. One loophole which many authorities exploited allowed them to use capital receipts to pay for repairs and maintenance despite this funding being against the spirit of the legislation.

iv. *The need for long term planning.* The frequent changes in legislation have meant that the 1980 system has not proved a stable framework within which long term capital programmes can be efficiently administered.

Other criticisms made of the system.   The fourth justification echoes one of the major criticisms aimed at the 1980 system by all concerned with the provision of housing. The need to produce a rolling programme for capital projects and for planning at least three to four years ahead was stressed earlier in this chapter. The year by year basis of HIP allocations is not compatible with this need; local authorities do not know how much they can spend on capital schemes from one year to the next and the problem can be exacerbated by changes to the HIP allocation announced within the year.

It is also argued that the restrictions on the use of capital receipts to enhance capital spending allocations reduces the incentive to sell assets. This is clearly true in the case of services which have the option to sell assets but may be less true for the housing service which is required to sell council houses to any tenant with 'the right to buy'. In practice the value of housing capital receipts (£12.5 billion out of the £17 billion raised from sale of assets during the years 1981/82 to 1987/88) may also provide a disincentive to other services to sell their assets. Under the 1980 system these services could benefit from the enforced sale of council houses in cases where the authority decides to use council house capital receipts to swell the capital spending powers of the other services, without having to lose any of their own assets.

The perceived inadequacies of the present system of local authority capital finance mentioned so far have focused, on the inadequacy of the distribution mechanism. That is how, once the spending power is determined by the Government, it is split between the 403 housing authorities. The system has also been criticised for damaging the housing service by delivering inadequate funding.

Between the years 1983/84 and 1987/88 gross capital spending on council housing in England and Wales dropped by about 22%, at a time when the Government's control on capital expenditure gave the authorities little choice in the matter. It is relatively simple to cut capital expenditure, as it usually represents the growth area of the organisation with implications for future jobs rather than present employment, but those cuts have long term effects on service provision. The enforced cuts in local government funding are seen by those who wish to preserve the local authority role of provider of housing as deeply damaging to the housing service and they point to increasing homelessness, the poor state of the housing stock and the reduced level of new build as proof of the inadequacy of the system. The Government's reply is that it is not satisfied with the present performance of local authorities and would prefer to see the housing service delivered by other organisations, and the increased constraints on capital borrowing made available to local authorities reflect this preference.

Successive Governments have applied some kind of control to local authority borrowings for at least the last 150 years, but it is only since 1980 that they have curtailed the local authority right to spend all the proceeds from asset sales on new capital schemes. At the end of 1987 local authorities had about £6 billion of net capital receipts that could have been used to finance capital schemes if the restrictions on capital spending had not existed. Local authorities are understandably indignant at being denied the full use of money they regard as their own.

The new system for control of capital expenditure

The 1990 system
The new system, initially outlined in the consultation paper *Local Government in England and Wales: Capital Expenditure and Finance* of 7 July 1988 will operate on four classes of capital expenditure:

  i.   the acquisition of the rights to use (other than on a temporary basis) land, buildings, plant, machinery, vehicles and other tangible fixed assets;
  ii. the construction of buildings, roads and other structures and any works which improves, enhances the value of, or lengthens the life of any property used by local authorities;
  iii. loans or grants given in support of the capital expenditure of others; and
  iv. long term investments.

There will be three sources of finance for this system:

  i.   borrowing or credit arrangements;
  ii. government grants or contributions from third parties, including other local authorities; and
  iii. the local authorities own resources, including contributions from current income and the proceeds of the sale of assets.

Borrowing and credit arrangements
At the beginning of the financial year each local authority will be told the amount of their 'basic credit approval'. The BCA will normally cover any category of capital expenditure which the local authority would normally incur. This BCA specifies the maximum capital expenditure that can be

financed from loan or credit arrangements. 'Credit arrangements' are those arrangements which while not borrowing in the accepted sense have the same economic effect as borrowing, that is of delaying payment for the asset from a fund held by the authority. Any expenditure financed from a credit arrangement, including finance leases, will normally be counted against the BCA for the year at 'the cash value of the total liability under the transaction'. A BCA will always be for a definite amount and relate to a particular year. When the BCAs are computed the government will take into account the authority's ability to pay its way using capital receipts. This means that some authorities could be assessed as having a negative BCA, in this case the authority will be notified that their BCA is nil. At the time that the authority is notified of its BCA for the year it will also be told the minimum level of BCA that will be made available for the next two years. Authorities may also be eligible for 'supplementary credit approval' (SCA) which will normally be given for particular categories of capital expenditure.

Local authority resources and contributions
The Government does not plan to take any action to control the amount of capital expenditure that local authorities pay for from their current revenue income, arguing that the controls inherent in the new community charge system (see Chapter 8) will be sufficient for their purposes. Local authorities are to be allowed to use only a portion of their proceeds from capital receipts to finance new capital expenditure, 25% of the proceeds of council house sales and 50% of any other capital receipts. The rest of the proceeds are to be used to redeem existing debt or finance 'credit arrangements'. The reason given for the lower percentage being applied to housing receipts is that in view of the imminent sales of council houses to private landlords, the housing service does not need the extra investment. The Government will require minimum debt repayment from revenue accounts (see Chapter 8).

The Local Government and Housing Act reinforces these proposals. The amount of borrowing power available to an authority in a year could be as shown in Figure 2.5.5.

	£mn
Basic Credit Approval	20.0
Supplementary Credit Approval	1.9
Proportion of capital receipts	
Housing (say 25% × £6mn)	1.5
Other (say 50% × £2mn)	1.0
Total spending controlled by Government	24.4
Additional funds from revenue sources	5.6
Total capital spending power	30.0

Figure 2.5.5

The authority would be free to set its own spending target, enhancing the Government's control target of £24.4mn by contributions from current income. The maximum the authority could borrow in the year to finance its capital spending would be £21.9mn, assuming that borrowing was its only form of 'credit arrangement'.

The implications for the housing service of the new capital controls proposed

The level of housing capital expenditure will be dependent on three things: how the BCA given to the authority is distributed between services, the extent to which the authority is prepared to finance capital from current housing income, and the amount of money raised in the year from the sale of housing assets. The BCA will be given to the authority as a whole, but its calculation is partly based on separate assessments of need made for each service including housing. These assessments will be called 'annual capital guidelines' and the Minister responsible for making the assessment will be required to notify the authority of the amount. The authority's BCA will be the sum of the service assessments less the extent to which the government expect the authority to finance its needs from its own capital receipts. The BCA can be spent on any allowable capital expenditure, the Council will take the responsibility for sharing it among services. The authority may also spend as much as it wishes from current housing income on housing capital expenditure. In practice this capital expenditure will have to be paid for from rent income. The authority can also use 25% of its housing capital receipts to pay for new capital expenditure.

Housing is also mentioned as the service most likely to become debt free in the near future. A housing authority disposing of all or a substantial part of its housing stock to private landlords may generate sufficient capital receipts not only to pay off all its debt and finance its remaining reduced capital programme but also to hand a surplus of capital receipts over to the county council to spend for the benefit of the area.

The new system – the way forward

The major changes to the capital expenditure control system if the current proposals are accepted are:
— a new definition of capital expenditure that does not include 'repairs and maintenance';
— the replacement of a power to borrow with a power to enter into credit arrangements;
— the removal of restrictions on the amount of capital expenditure that can be financed from revenue funds;
— the requirement to set aside a proportion of capital receipts to repay old debt or finance new credit agreements;

— the introduction of credit approvals that take the financial resources of individual local authorities into consideration.

The proposed system seems to offer at least two improvements on the current system, it aims for a fairer distribution of borrowing power and it offers some assistance in forward planning. The fairer distribution of borrowing power however, depends on the ability of the Government to produce a system that can accurately estimate capital receipts for individual authorities and this type of income is notoriously difficult to predict. The production of minimum BCAs for two years ahead takes some of the uncertainty out of the planning system but must also make it difficult to plan the use of the possible marginal increases in funding announced at the beginning of a financial year.

Conclusion

This chapter has considered the financing of housing production expenditure and the constraints upon such spending by Government controls and the conflicting needs of other services. One further constraint needs to be considered, the ability of the authority to pay the running costs of the assets acquired by production spending. The financing of housing revenue expenditure and the constraint this financing can put on the capital spending for the service will be discussed in Chapter 8.

Part 3
Revenue finance

Chapter 6
Owner occupation

This chapter will discuss the idea that an owner occupied house is an item of investment which generates for its owner an 'imputed' income in the form of a stream of housing services. It will also distinguish between this theoretical notion of 'imputed' income generated by the dwelling and the household's 'disposable' income which is largely derived from employment and is received as a stream of money. It will make the point that, in practice, it is part of this disposable money income which is used to pay for the day-to-day costs of being an owner occupier. The chapter will further consider the way in which owner occupation is treated for fiscal purposes.

The second part of the chapter will consider the main items of housing revenue expenditure facing the owner occupier. These will be identified as loan charges, maintenance costs and management costs.

Revenue income and expenditure

As managers of their houses, owner occupiers are responsible for meeting all the revenue charges, or 'costs-in-use', associated with the dwellings they own. In other words, they are responsible for all the recurring charges made with respect to interest and debt redemption on mortgage or other loans taken out to acquire their properties, together with all the payments made for the purpose of maintaining and repairing the fabric of the houses once they have been acquired.

In practice, the day-to-day revenue expenses of owner occupation are met out of the household's total disposable income which is generally derived from employment earnings and any borrowing or welfare benefits to which they are entitled. However, in its strictest sense, the housing revenue income of an owner occupier stems from his or her ownership of the house as an asset and should be thought of as the revenue benefit that accrues in the form of an income in kind. This benefit in kind (housing services) is often referred to as *imputed rent* or *imputed income*.

We will now consider revenue income and expenditure in detail.

Revenue income

As with the case of housing organisations such as housing associations and local authorities, owner occupiers can be said to receive incomes which are derived from, or related to, the dwellings they own. Also, like housing organisations, owner occupiers receive these incomes in the form of 'rents' and 'subsidies'. The difference between the housing income of an owner occupier and that of a housing organisation is that the 'rent' is not paid by a tenant but is thought of as an *imputed income* which the owner receives from 'letting' the property to him or herself. The owner occupier receives revenue income subsidies in the form of tax concessions through the non-payment of 'schedule A' income tax (which is the schedule dealing with income from land and property) and through the receipt of 'Mortgage Interest Relief' where the house is being purchased by means of a loan (see Figure 3.6.1).

Imputed rental income
As we have already indicated, in a strict economic sense, the housing revenue income of an owner occupier should be thought of as that income which is directly derived from his or her ownership of the property. An owner of a house may either let it out to another person

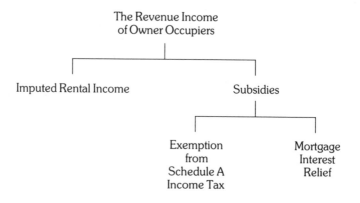

Figure 3.6.1

or occupy it as his or her own home. If the owner lets it out, the rental income he or she receives after allowances will be taxed as part of his or her income. If, on the other hand, the owner chooses to live in the house as an owner occupier, he or she receives a benefit which can be thought of as an *income in kind*, and this benefit is not subject to income taxation. In short, a house can be thought of as a durable asset which yields a flow of untaxed housing services which are consumed by the owner occupant. The term 'imputed income' is used to describe these services because it is a (non-monetary) financial benefit which is not physically received in the form of a payment from a second party.

It is possible of course, for an owner occupier to take in a lodger or let out part of the house, say the garage. In such circumstances, the owner would receive actual revenue income from the house in addition to the imputed rent income.

Revenue subsidies to owner occupation
1. The non-taxation of imputed income.   Prior to 1963 owner occupied dwellings were treated for tax purposes as investments. The imputed income benefit received was taxed under Schedule A Income Tax (see above), certain costs, including that of servicing the mortgage loan, being granted as allowances. In these circumstances *mortgage interest tax relief* cannot be regarded as a subsidy. Such relief is quite simply a legitimate tax allowance set against investment earnings and, as such, is on a par with similar allowances in the business world.

While income of this nature is still taxed in a number of countries including France, Germany, Belgium and the Netherlands, it is no longer taxed in Britain. By no longer subjecting an owner occupier's imputed housing income to taxation, the Inland Revenue is treating the house as an item of personal *consumption* rather than an investment.

The reason that owner occupied houses were exempted from Schedule A income taxation in 1963 was largely political and related to the rating revaluation that took place in that year. The tax was assessed on the assumed market letting value of the house net of repairs and maintenance, and rateable values were used as the basis of the assessment. However, houses were only periodically revalued for rating purposes, and at the time, the 1936/37 rating valuations were being used. A rating revaluation took place in 1963 and, if the Schedule A tax had remained, it would have meant that, in many areas, the burden would have trebled or quadrupled. This would have had damaging political consequences for the Government at a time when more and more of the electorate were becoming owner occupiers[1].

The changed tax position of owner occupiers in this respect put them in a privileged position and made the allowance of mortgage interest relief anomalous. As we saw in Chapter 3 this privileged position is reinforced by the fact that capital gains tax is not levied on the appreciation in value of an owner's only or main residence. The existence of these privileges has led to a number of commentators suggesting that owner occupation is treated inconsistently in the tax system[2]. Other taxable forms of investment are usually subject to tax on both income and any capital gains accruing. A private landlord, for example, is taxed on both rental income and capital gains. Such a landlord can offset expenses, including any interest payment on a mortgage loan, against that tax liability. In contrast, the owner occupier receives this interest relief but pays no tax on imputed income or on capital gains. It might be argued that such privileges offend against the basic taxation principles of 'equity' and 'neutrality'.

2. *Mortgage interest tax relief.*   Owner occupiers are eligible to receive income tax relief at their marginal tax rates on the interest element of their monthly mortgage payments. This means that the relief is given at the individual's highest rate of income tax. Before 1983 this relief was granted by means of the Inland Revenue adjusting the borrower's personal tax coding or assessment. This system was changed in 1983 with the introduction of a scheme known as *Mortgage Interest Relief at Source* (MIRAS).

MIRAS and basic rate taxpayers. Under the MIRAS scheme, basic rate taxpayers now pay the monthly interest on their mortgage loans net of tax. The scheme works as follows. The mortgagee (lender) calculates the borrower's periodic repayments, which, in the case of a *repayment mortgage* (see Chapter 3), will include elements of interest and capital. The lender then works out the tax relief at the basic rate on the interest element, and the mortgagor (borrower) makes a payment comprised of capital and interest less basic rate tax.

Example

Assume a repayment mortage with a nominal monthly repayment of £300 made up of £270 interest and £30 capital, and also assume basic rate of income tax is 25%.

Actual monthly repayment calculated as:

Interest	£270.00
Capital	£30.00
Total	£300.00
Less tax on interest, £270 at 25%	£67.50
Net monthly payment	*£232.50*

In this way, under the MIRAS scheme, basic rate tax is deducted from the payments made to the lender, so that the basic rate taxpayer does not have to claim the tax back from the Inland Revenue.

MIRAS and higher rate taxpayers

For a higher rate taxpayer, relief is allowed against his or her higher rate of tax. This means that basic rate tax is still deducted from the payments to the lender and the borrower then obtains the extra relief due above the basic rate through an adjustment to his or her tax code or annual tax assessment. A tax code adjustment involves the Inland Revenue receiving an estimate of the gross interest chargeable on the loan for the tax year. At the end of the year they may require a confirmation of the amount of interest actually paid. Building societies give this information direct to the Inland Revenue. When borrowing from other types of institution, the mortgagor may have to supply this information on a form obtainable from the lender.

The conditions of Mortgage Interest Tax Relief (MITR)
The mortgage interest tax relief concession is subject to a number of limitations.

— The loan must relate to the borrower's main domestic residence.
— There is a limit to the size of mortgage which qualifies for relief: the relief limit is confirmed or changed each year in the Budget. At present (tax year 1988/89) the relief is allowed only on the first £30,000 of outstanding loan.
— Since the 1988 Budget the £30,000 limit is applied to the residence rather than, as hitherto, to the borrower, so that the joint mortgagors can no longer each claim a £30,000 exemption but have to share the exemption between them.
— Since the 1984 Budget, the premium payments on endowment policies do not qualify for tax relief (but the interest element does).
— Since the 1988 Budget the mortgage interest relief is restricted to loans for the *purchase* of homes, and relief on loans for *home improvements* no longer applies.
— Since the 1988 Budget, loans taken out for the purchase of a home for a dependent relative or former or separated spouse, no longer qualify for tax relief.
— Owners may not qualify for relief if they have some special exemption from UK tax on their earnings: for example, because they work for a foreign government.

The case for and against MITR
As indicated above, mortgage tax relief was originally justified as a legitimate tax allowance set against the payment of Schedule A income tax. With the abandonment of such a tax liability for owner occupiers, it could no longer be justified on those grounds. Those supporting the retention of MITR now tend to justify their position in different and more general terms. They readily accept that the concession discriminates positively in favour of owner occupiers, but argue that this is 'no bad thing' as it acts to encourage home ownership. In other words, its retention is most strongly argued by those who are politically committed to the 'market agenda' in general and to the development of a 'property-owning democracy' in particular.

In recent years, however, a number of academics and housing practitioners have challenged the efficacy of mortgage interest relief concessions for owner occupiers. The case against relief in its present form rests on an argument that it is both unfair and inefficient.

It is seen as unfair in that it gives the greatest benefit to those with the largest mortgages (up to the maximum limit of £30,000) and to those with the highest marginal tax rates. As the recent Inquiry into British Housing[3] reported, Treasury figures indicate that owners on higher than average incomes receive a disproportionate amount of relief, indicating that the assistance is broadly regressive.

MITR is seen by some as inefficient in opportunity cost terms. That is, it is argued that the tax foregone by the Exchequer (some £4 billion in 1988) could be more effectively utilised on some other aspects of housing or welfare policy. This point has been made by numerous practitioners, academics and commentators including the Duke of Edinburgh's Inquiry into British Housing, the Association of District Councils and the Royal Institution of Chartered Surveyors[4]. Although the present Conservative Government is committed to the maintenance of MITR there are signs (from press reports) that consideration has been given to making the scheme less regressive by restricting relief to standard rate taxpayers.

Household disposable income, grants and loan finance

In practice the revenue expenses of owner occupation are met out of a household's total disposable income and savings which are generally derived from employment earnings and/or any welfare benefits to which they are entitled. Larger items of repair and maintenance may possibly be financed by taking out a loan and some work may attract grant aid. The various grants available to owner occupiers are discussed in Chapter 5.

Until recently the most tax efficient way of borrowing money for home maintenance purposes has been by extending an existing mortgage by taking out a 'top-up loan'. These are sometimes referred to as 'further advances' and until 1988, qualified for mortgage interest tax relief so long as the borrower's total mortgage did not exceed the £30,000 limit. This concession was discontinued in the 1988 Budget. It was withdrawn because of evidence that many of the advances were being used on non-essential maintenance or even for non-housing purposes altogether, such as buying a car, financing holidays or paying off higher interest debts.

Government policy and the revenue costs of owner occupation

Recent measures have concentrated on getting people onto the ladder of home ownership and have paid little or no attention to the problems related to sustaining owner occupation. Government policy has focused on the issue of *becoming* rather than the issue of *being* an owner occupier. As Valerie Karn et al. have observed, the measures seem to have been introduced

> "regardless of the consequences and in doing so, it demonstrates a disturbing belief in the bounteous and unproblematic nature of home ownership."[5]

One clear area of concern relates to the conspicuous lack of provision of support for low income owners in relation to the upkeep of their homes. This concern is sharpened by the fact that, as a generalisation, lower income owners tend to inhabit older properties many of which are in a poor state of repair.

As well as a reduction in grant expenditure and a cutting back of area-based improvement programmes, general fiscal changes have served to diminish financial incentives for owners to maintain and repair their houses. In 1984 value added tax was imposed on building alterations and as mentioned above, in 1988, tax relief on the interest payments on home improvement loans was abolished.

In addition to these specific concerns, it might be argued that the fiscal arrangements as a whole militate against an effective process of home maintenance. By focusing Exchequer help on MIRAS and the issue of entry to owner occupation, policy has tended to stimulate consumption and demand rather than production and supply, with a consequential stimulation of house prices and a reduction of activity relating to the frequency and quality of house improvement and repair.

The new Local Government Finance Act will bring in a new system of improvement grants from April 1990. A Consultation Paper has been produced in advance of the Act under the title *Home Improvement Policy: Consultation Paper*, 1989. This indicates the Government's intention to target grants towards lower income households by a means test linked to the housing benefit system. Anyone with an income up to £20 above the level used to calculate housing benefit (the applicable amount) will receive full grant. Above this level owner occupiers will be required to contribute 20p of every extra pound they earn towards paying off the cost of improvement.

In 1989 the Government estimated that 3.4 million owner occupiers lived in sub-standard properties (based on the English House Condition Survey). It is expected that only some 1.3 million will be eligible for grant aid under the new arrangements, and of these, many may well be deterred by the level of household contribution demanded. In short, the encouragement of the expansion of owner occupation has not been matched by a similar increase in the amount of public resources being devoted to maintenance or housing renewal.

Revenue expenditure

The main revenue expenditure for owner occupiers relates to loan charges and maintenance costs. In addition, prudent owners take out insurance to cover the structure of the property against being damaged or destroyed.

1. Loan charges
Because of the high cost of housing relative to family savings and disposable incomes, only a limited number of owner occupied houses are bought outright for cash: the typical purchase is in part financed by a mortgage loan (see Chapter 3). This means that for many owners, a

major item of revenue expenditure takes the form of repayments of loan principal and payments of interest.

The real burden of debt. The amount payable by way of loan charges depends upon (a) the size of the loan, (b) the period of repayment, (c) the current rate of interest charged, and (d) the amount of mortgage interest tax relief received.

(a) The size of the loan will be subject to restrictions set by the mortgagee's lending policy. This will be based on an assessment of the property's value and the mortgagor's ability to meet the repayments. As far as the property is concerned, the lender will take into account its age, state of repair and location. Any assessment of the borrower's capacity to repay will normally take into account such factors as his or her age, income and prospects of income. As explained in Chapter 3, increases in competition in the mortgage market have had the effect of liberalising lending policies in recent years and lending institutions have become more flexible with regard to their assessments.

Most house purchasers seeking loan finance turn to a commercial finance institution such as a building society or a bank. In the case of secure tenants purchasing their homes under the 'Right to Buy' provisions of the Housing statutes, they have the additional option of a mortgage from the vendor landlord, in which case, ability to pay is still taken into account by reference to a loan-income ratio. However, as in the private finance sector, scope for flexibility exists and the vendor landlord may, if the tenant agrees, treat the tenant as entitled to a mortgage in excess of that which would be determined by the ratio (so long as it does not exceed the purchase price plus certain associated costs).

(b) The period over which repayments are spread is usually limited to a maximum of 40 years, although a shorter term of (say) 25 years is more typical. Because of concern about ability to pay in the future as well as in the present, many lenders will set the term to end before or soon after the mortgagor reaches retirement age.

(c) As far as interest rates are concerned, under the provisions of the Consumer Credit Act 1974, these have to be advertised in terms of the *annual percentage rate* (APR) which indicates the true and full yearly cost of servicing the loan. The requirement to display the APR prominently in mortgage advertisements is intended to allow potential borrowers to compare the costs of loans on a common basis and thereby make an informed choice. When interest rates rise during the term of the mortgage, most lenders will generally allow an extension of the borrowing period as an alternative to an increase in the periodic repayments.

(d) Mortgage interest tax relief has the effect of reducing the real cost of indebtedness to the borrower and is discussed in detail above in the section dealing with Revenue Income.

As well as the factors mentioned so far, the real burden of a mortgage is also affected by the interaction between *inflation* and the *historic cost* of the loan. At certain times and in certain areas, house price inflation may be ahead of the general rate of increase in prices and incomes, and this can cause problems of overcommitment for some owners. Such problems are most likely to affect lower income, first-time buyers in high house-price areas who are in the early stages of their mortgage term. Research shows that in recent years younger owners have been committing, on average, between 25 and 30 per cent of their disposable incomes for the purchase of terraced houses and 30 per cent or more for flats and maisonettes. In high price areas such as Greater London and the South East of England, these proportions are even higher[6]. However, because the loan is fixed at the time of purchase, repayments relate to 'historic' rather than to 'replacement' costs, and this means that inflation will tend to reduce the real burden of payments over time. In addition, the real burden of servicing the mortgage loan is further reduced for most by the favourable tax treatment of owner occupiers as discussed above.

2. Maintenance costs

The second major category of revenue expense confronting owner occupiers is that which stems from the need to maintain their homes in a state of good repair.

The distinction between 'primary maintenance' and 'improvement'.

Primary maintenance work is undertaken to prevent or arrest the building's structure and fabric from deteriorating and is therefore concerned with maintaining the condition of the building envelope. In other words, primary maintenance is carried out to ensure that the building is 'safe and sound'. This type of maintenance might occur in response to some form of unexpected structural failure or it might be planned and budgeted for in advance. Improvement work is undertaken to add to the building's size or quality rather than to maintain it in working order. This may involve building some kind of extension to the house or converting it to a different use (e.g. into flats), installing some feature or facility it previously lacked, or refurbishing it to bring it up to some higher standard of accommodation. In this way, improvement works can be said to be adding to the capital value of the dwelling rather than simply maintaining its value.

In Chapter 1 a theoretical distinction was made between 'capital' and 'revenue' finance. It was made clear that in theory capital finance is used to add to the quantity or quality of the housing stock and revenue finance is used to maintain the stock in a reasonable state of repair. On this basis, 'maintenance' can be thought of as requiring revenue finance and 'improvement' can be thought of as requiring capital finance. In financial practice, however, the distinction between 'primary maintenance' and 'improvement' can be blurred. Some primary maintenance work, such as a major roof repair or the reinforcing of foundations to arrest subsidence, may require as much or more money than some improvement work such as installing central heating, and also, like much improvement work, some primary maintenance jobs may qualify for grant aid or require loan finance. In other words, improvements and primary maintenance works may be financed in similar ways and from similar sources.

The distinction between 'primary' and 'secondary maintenance'. In contrast to primary maintenance, secondary maintenance is carried out more on a day-to-day basis and includes repair of non-structural elements. It includes non-essential external redecoration and nearly all internal redecoration as well as the various minor jobs around the house. Most do-it-yourself (DIY) activity falls into the category of secondary maintenance. Whether carried out by a contractor or on a DIY basis, these activities are typically paid for out of current income or savings rather than by means of a grant or loan.

Factors affecting the level of maintenance. The amount of money an owner occupier spends on maintenance over a period will be affected by (a) his or her financial resources and priorities, (b) the age of the building and the 'wear and tear' to which it is subjected, (c) the owner's ability and inclination to do work him or herself on the property, (d) the quality of the building and the nature and quality of previous improvement and maintenance work, and (e) the way the market values maintenance work. We will say something briefly about each of these.

(a) The primary element of a household's financial resources is its disposable income. Because houses are costly to repair, low income households are likely to suffer poor housing conditions in the absence of government aid. In this way, it may be argued that 'housing decay is one manifestation of poverty'[7].

As we saw in Chapter 3, recent governments have done much to encourage entry to owner occupation. In particular, since 1979, there has been a series of measures aimed principally at those who, in the past, would not have considered owning their own homes. In addition to specific policies aimed at low income households, the decline in expenditure on public sector rented housing (see Chapter 2) combined with the continual shrinkage in the availability of privately rented accommodation must have served to force large numbers of people into owner occupation through a lack of appropriate housing alternatives. Many of these will have been low income households who have many demands on their limited resources and who, as a result, may choose to 'under-maintain' their houses (i.e. maintain them to a level which is below the minimum standard deemed desirable by government policy) in order to release funds for other domestic purposes.

In higher income households, maintenance also has to compete with other budget items. In any household, what actually gets spent on maintenance will, to a large extent, depend upon the priority it is given over the other claims on the household's savings and disposable income. In other words, money spent on the house will have an *opportunity cost* in the form of the sacrifices of some other household need or demand. In the case of a relatively wealthy family, living in a well maintained house, the sacrifice may have only a limited effect on their lifestyle: it might, for example involve reduced savings for a short period or less expensive holidays for a year or two. However, in the case of a low income family living in an older, poorly maintained house, the sacrifice needed to repair it to a satisfactory standard may involve a considerable reduction in their general standard of living over an extended period.

With the reduction in grant expenditure and the curtailing of the area-based improvement programmes, owner occupiers have been increasingly placed in the position of having to rely more and more on their own resources. There are considerable difficulties in obtaining meaningful information on how much home owners spend on repairs and maintenance. This is partly because only a limited amount of research has been done on the topic and partly because researchers have found that owners do not usually keep records of such expenditure. Furthermore, much of the maintenance work is done on a 'do-it-yourself' (DIY) basis or by someone else working within the informal economy. Researchers in this field find that the problem is further compounded by the fact that most owners find it very difficult to cost work done by themselves or by friends or relatives. However recent research relating to a sample of low income owners occupying pre-1919, poor quality terraced housing in Bristol indicated that between 1981 and 1986 such households spent an average of some £3,000 per house. In this particular study, two thirds of total expenditure came from private sources and a third from grants[8].

(b) It is self-evidently true that buildings decay through time and use: accordingly, the annual maintenance costs associated with a house tend to increase as the building ages. In this respect, it is of general interest that in most regions of Britain over 25 per cent of the housing stock was built before 1919. In Wales, where the level of owner occupation is above average, the proportion of the stock built before 1919 is as high as 40 per cent[9].

(c) Another factor affecting the level of maintenance in this sector is the knowledge, skill and inclination of owners to do or to organise maintenance work themselves. In other words, resources other than finance will be available to some households. Where it exists, household expertise and energy can be combined with finance to carry out certain maintenance tasks. However, it is difficult for home owners to acquire substantial experience in maintenance: few will ever undertake specific major jobs, like a roof replacement, and of those who do, very few indeed will *reuse* the maintenance experience and expertise gained. This contrasts with professional housing agencies, such as local authorities or housing associations, who continually accumulate and reuse such knowledge.

One form of direct help currently being developed is *agency services* which aim to offer technical advice and limited financial assistance to home owners who are either elderly or who live in specific geographical areas. As owner occupation expands, it would be useful for such services to develop more widely and act as reservoirs of experience and knowledge for owner occupiers to draw upon.

(d) The nature and quality of previous building and maintenance work can affect current and future maintenance costs. To some extent this relates to the points made in (a) and (c) above. That is, some owners may 'under-maintain' through choice or ignorance. From the point of view of a professional builder, surveyor or housing manager, some private owners may decide to carry out maintenance work in the 'wrong' way. In other words, it may be that some owners create future maintenance problems by doing maintenance jobs in an inappropriate sequence, in an inappropriate way, with inappropriate materials or by employing an inappropriate contractor. The use of the word 'inappropriate' here is intended to indicate a situation in which conventionally accepted 'good practice' by a local authority or housing association would have resulted in things being done differently.

(e) The way the housing market operates tends to militate against providing owners with an incentive to maintain the structure of their properties in accordance with conventionally accepted 'good practice'. More precisely it tends to discourage owners from undertaking one type of work while encouraging them to undertake another. Owners' decisions are based both on consumption needs and their perceptions of the investment potential of the dwellings they possess. The housing market seems to operate in a way that emphasises the value of decorative work relating to the visible fabric (painting, kitchen fittings, etc.) rather than to primary maintenance work relating to the building's structure. In other words, market weaknesses in the form of imperfect buyer knowledge, may affect the rational maintenance behaviour of owners so as to emphasise short-term consumption goals relating to the appearance of the house rather than the long-term investment goals relating to the physical life of the building.

Furthermore, where house prices are depressed, maintenance may be neglected as the costs may not be recouped in the resale value of the property. Where prices are rising, more owners may be encouraged to improve their dwellings, but, on the other hand, it also makes economic sense for them to downgrade maintenance in order to increase their 'profit margin' or 'yield' as house prices reflect location factors rather than house conditions. This market phenomenon is sometimes referred to as *the valuation gap* and offers an economic explanation for 'under-maintenance'. It is called *the valuation gap* because it draws attention to a presumed shortfall between the market value of a house after maintenance or improvement and its pre-improved value plus improvement costs.

3. 'Management' costs
In the case of owner occupation, most supervision and management costs are counted in time rather than money terms. The main item in the latter category is normally the cost of insurance. Although there is no legal obligation for an owner occupied dwelling to be insured against damage or destruction, a prudent owner will take out appropriate cover and all lending institutions insist on such cover before approving a mortgage loan. Policies vary in terms of cover provided and premiums to be paid, but all will be based on a calculation of value which relates to the costs of replacement rather than to the purchase price. Because the rebuilding costs of a house are frequently in excess of its market value, owners often have to insure their properties for a larger amount than its potential sale price. Most insurance companies provide index-linked policies in which the sum insured and premiums automatically rise in line with rebuilding cost inflation.

Notes and references

1 As well as exempting owner occupation, the Finance Act 1963 altered the whole way in which Schedule A tax was assessed. Before the 1963 Budget the tax had been charged on an annual value related to the rateable value. After the 1963 Budget the taxation of income from land and buildings (Schedule A) was based on the actual profit arising (i.e. receipts less allowable expenditure).

2 See for example, *Inquiry into British Housing: Report*, Chairman HRH The Duke of Edinburgh, NHFA 1985, p. 11.

3 *Inquiry into British Housing: Report.* Ibid. pp. 11–12. The Report took figures from Hansard indicating that in 1983/84, 9 per cent of those receiving MITR were on incomes of £20,000 or above and they received 19 per cent of the total relief.

4 NFHA (1986) op. cit. *Foundations for future housing*, ADC, 1987; RICS *Housing in the Eighties*, 1986.

5 Karn V., Kemeney J. and Williams P., *Home Ownership in the Inner City*, in Booth P. and Crook T. (eds) *Low Cost Home Ownership*, Gower, p. 150.

6 Walker A., *Housing Taxation: Owner Occupation and the Reform of Housing Finance*, CHAS Occasional Paper 9, 1986, Chapter 2.

7 Building Economic Development Committee, *Ways to Better Housing*, NEDO, 1986, p. 19.

8 Mackintosh S, Malpass P, and Garnett D., *Most Peoples' Dream: A study of Home Ownership and the Management of Maintenance of Older Low Cost Housing*, NAB/Bristol Polytechnic, 1988.

9 *Inquiry into British Housing: Supplement*, Information Paper 8, Table 2, p. xxviii, NFHA. 1986.

Chapter 7
Revenue finance and the independent rented sector

In Chapter 4 we looked at the ways in which money capital is used to provide housing for rent outside the municipal sector. In this chapter we will consider the day-to-day revenue expenses generated within 'independent' rented housing, and how such expenses are financed. In other words, this chapter is concerned with the management of rented housing in the independent sector, rather than its provision.

Once it has been built or acquired, rented housing is managed in a way that helps further the particular objectives of the owner. In the case of a private landlord, for example, this involves letting and maintaining the property with the primary intention of generating a level of income which guarantees a financial return on the initial capital investment. In the case of a housing association, until now, this has also involved letting and maintaining the property with the primary intention of generating income. However, as housing associations are concerned primarily with the pursuit of social objectives, they have not so far sought to maximise profits, but instead have concentrated upon maximising social benefits.

Whether a profit-seeking landlord or a socially-responsible housing association, both require revenue income to meet their various management costs and to cover any outstanding capital loan repayments. Nonetheless, different management objectives and styles result in different revenue costs being incurred, and in different approaches to revenue income. Here we differentiate between three broad strands of non-municipal rented housing management, which have differing management objectives, together with the financial arrangements which underpin them.

1. Private rented housing
The management of private rented housing is influenced by property interests which are dominated by objectives which relate to the

generation of financial returns. These returns can be of a capital nature, in the form of capital appreciation, or of a revenue nature, in the form of rental income. Revenue returns or 'profits' are dependent upon the relationship between rents received and outgoings. Thus, 'profit-maximising' landlords will seek to charge a rent which is as high as the market will bear, or the law will allow, while at the same time keeping their costs to the minimum necessary to maintain the capital value of the property.

2. Subsidised housing association activity

The property interests of housing associations in receipt of government subsidies are dominated by the need to combine social objectives which relate to the notion of responding to needs in society, with sound management organised around the principles of 'value for money' rather than 'maximisation of profit'. Like any commercial organisation, housing associations are concerned with maintaining the value of their capital assets and operating efficiently and effectively.

3. The new regime: housing association activity generated using private funding

In Chapter 4 we discussed the development of housing association schemes which have been funded through a combination of public and private funds. The changes to the system of HAG and the introduction of mixed funding, along with the abolition of Fair Rents, mean that more housing associations are likely to use varying amounts of private finance, leaving the more heavily subsidised branch of activity to assume a stronger 'welfare' role. At the same time, as the take-up of private finance to assist with the capital costs of provision becomes more common, so there will be pressures to adopt management practices which reassure private investors on the 'safety' of their investment. This means ensuring not only that the investment holds its value, but also that the combination of the investment and the way in which the association manages it are capable of producing a financial return. For the association, a return is needed in order to meet the interest charges payable on loans which they have raised from the private sector.

The success of mixed funding schemes depends upon private investors having confidence in the abilities of associations to meet these charges. With the abolition of Fair Rents and the requirement that housing associations set 'affordable rents' which reflect the real costs of provision and management of their property, private investors are likely to be reassured on this point.

In the following sections we will consider the systems of revenue funding and financial control operating in each of these housing categories.

Private rented housing

Managing agents

Private landlordism takes many organisational forms. It may take the form of a small scale operation run by an individual owner letting out a room, part of a house, a whole investment property or a number of houses. Landlords operating at this end of the scale employ no staff to carry out management and consequently they have low overheads, as management costs are kept to a minimum. Other than costs incurred on maintenance, the main revenue costs for small landlords relate to professional services, such as legal and accounting fees.

One step up from the small landlord are the agents who act for people who wish to let property. The principle behind property management services is that an agent manages rented property on the owner's behalf in return for a fee or a sum retained from the rental revenue. There are many types of managing agent, some with a high degree of professionalism, others badly organised and, as recent reports have suggested, even fraudulent[1]. Typical examples of managing agencies include those which are established as secondary to the main function of firms or businesses involved in estate agency, surveying, or the provision of legal and accounting services. Independent accommodation agencies, involved in finding property for clients who wish to rent, also sometimes act for property owners.

In addition to self-managing owners and their agents, landlord–investors — individuals, but more usually corporate bodies — both own and manage portfolios of properties which may contain residential, commercial or industrial property investments. Management of property on this rather larger scale is carried out by companies whose primary skills are in investment management rather than housing management.

The financial objectives of private landlords

The private landlord receives a revenue income in the form of rent, and, like any property owner, incurs revenue expenditure in relation to the management of their property. Landlords take both a long-term and a short-term view of their financial objectives and these perspectives are reflected in the way in which they treat revenue income and expenditure.

Long term objectives   are focused on the likely value of the property as a capital asset at some point in the future. Long term financial objectives are therefore specifically investment objectives, as the landlord-investor will want to see an improvement in the capital value of the property during the period of the investment. They are most likely to be framed around landlords' requirements that, upon disposal of the property, the principal sum originally invested, along with a sum representing the value added to the property during the term of the investment, be returned to them in the disposal price.

Long term objectives may be pursued *directly* through the management strategy adopted by the landlord, or alternatively they may *indirectly* influence the decision making arena within which the landlord-investor operates.

In the first case, landlords have a wide range of direct opportunities for pursuing management aims which reflect the objective of maintaining and protecting the value of their capital investment. For example, where a landlord buys a property on a leasehold basis, as would be the case with a flat located within a larger development, it might make good sense, if the opportunity arises, to buy out the freehold. Alternatively, if the property were a block of flats or adjoined other properties, it might similarly make sense to buy up some of the adjoining property, thus extending the portfolio in a cost-effective way. Where flats or houses fall vacant during the term of the investment, it might be appropriate to alter the tenancy arrangements, perhaps reletting on a short term or fixed term basis.

On the second point, the factors which indirectly influence landlords' decisions about management tend to be about the state of the property market and the role played by taste in fashioning that market. For example, landlords may own rented housing in an area of a town which becomes unfashionable to the type of consumer they wish to attract. Alternatively, landlords providing cheap rented housing might find their property is situated too far away from a college whose students they wish to attract. Under such circumstances, the landlord faced with the problem of deciding what to do to restore the property's revenue-earning capacity, might be prompted to sell, or convert and upgrade, or even redevelop it to serve a new non-residential function.

Short term objectives are reflected in the way day-to-day management is organised, and they are conceived with long term objectives in mind. Management is funded through revenue income, and revenue income comprises principally rent received. The amount of rental income received will depend upon the landlord's attitude towards and management of rent collection, the rent levels set and how frequently these are reviewed, and decisions relating to the number of tenancies created in the property.

The day-to-day revenue expenditure incurred as a result of management activity includes the cost of repairs and insurance cover for the property, as well as the costs of employing staff, maintaining an office, and paying for professional services. Also part of revenue expenditure are costs relating to the enforcement of the tenancy conditions, including for example any action needed to recover rent arrears. Landlords make individual business decisions on all of these items, and these decisions have consequences for levels of expenditure.

Both the long and short term objectives adopted by landlords therefore, determine how much money they decide to spend on their property. In general terms, items of expenditure which relate to long-term objectives are met out of capital; while items of expenditure which relate to short-term management objectives are met out of revenue.

The revenue income of private landlords

Private landlords raise their revenue from three basic sources. These are (in order of their overall importance): rents collected, deposits or premiums collected in conjunction with the setting up of new tenancies, and the imposition and collection of service charges.

1. Rent   From 1989 in line with the provisions of the 1988 Housing Act, private landlords (as well as housing associations, as will be shown later) setting up new tenancies have been able to charge market rents on their property. In the case of those tenancies governed by the Rent Acts which were set up before the 1988 Housing Act, landlords continue to charge and apply for registration of a Fair Rent for their property until the tenancy is ended, or the property sold to a new landlord. Only when this happens can market rents be introduced. In the case of tenancies protected under the Rent Acts, where a rent has been agreed between landlord and tenant without it ever being registered, the tenant continues to have security of tenure, and both parties must continue to agree the rent until the tenancy ends. In other words, in law, such landlords cannot charge a market rent, and it is still permissible for a Fair Rent to be registered for the property. In reality of course, the real difference between an 'agreed rent' and a market rent may be marginal. In effect, this means that market rents will operate alongside 'agreed rents' and Fair Rents for a period, before they replace them altogether.

The Fair Rent System which continues to operate in conjunction with some tenancies which are protected under the terms of the 1977 Rent Act, is administered by the Rent Officer Service. Rent Officers are independent officials, neither part of central nor local government, whose activities are nonetheless overseen by the Department of the Environment, which funds their activities.

In registering a Fair Rent, Rent Officers follow general guidelines which require them to make a qualitative assessment of rent for an individual property. Their assessment must take account of the age and condition of the dwelling, local amenities and the immediate environment, and the furnishings and level of services provided with the tenancy. At the same time, the figure which they propose must be arrived at after consideration of both the landlord's and the tenant's views, though not their financial circumstances. Both landlord and tenant have the right to appeal against the figure proposed. The landlord may charge the new rent as soon as it is registered, and may apply for a reregistration every two years.

In Chapter 4 we referred to the problems caused by restrictions on rental income which have affected private landlords' attitudes to continuing in business in the private rented accommodation sector. The levels of Fair Rents set by Rent Officers are said to have resulted in an ever-decreasing yield to private landlords over the last decade, with the argument being put forward that Fair Rents as a form of rent control have only served to increase the housing shortage by discouraging new private rented provision.

Market rents are associated with the establishment of assured tenancies. In practice, market rents involve the landlord setting a figure which the market will bear; this may imply little more than the landlord setting a rent which is in line with local rents for rented accommodation, and then finding a tenant who is willing to pay that price. Additional considerations revolve around what could loosely be termed the landlord's pricing policy: the anticipated level of periodic costs likely to be incurred by maintenance, the level of outgoings on items such as loan repayments, and the level of profit sought by the landlord. All of these factors have a bearing on the landlord's calculation of the total revenue which must be raised in order to make the initial investment pay. The total revenue required is thus reflected in rent levels. Tenants have rights of appeal against rent increases in the case of assured tenancies, and against 'excessive rents' in the case of assured shorthold tenancies.

2. *Deposits and premiums*   In spite of the 1977 Rent Act attempt to outlaw deposits and premiums, many landlords continued to ask for such payments from prospective tenants before awarding a tenancy. This is probably because the letter of the law was unclear and the demand for rented accommodation has always been such that many people will not challenge a demand for an additional payment when this is in effect the key to their obtaining accommodation.

The 1988 Housing Act effectively lifts restrictions on landlords making such charges, and where prior to 1989 landlords could only safely charge *returnable* deposits, they may now make a non-returnable charge in the form of a premium, known alternatively as 'key-money'. Whether returnable or otherwise, landlords thus have the use of these funds for the duration of the tenancy, having made a choice about retaining all or some of the sum when the tenancy ends.

Deposits and premiums act as a barrier to entry to rented accommodation for low income households, particularly for households whose main income is in the form of state benefits. The speed of the transaction may not give a low income household sufficient time to raise the money required to secure the tenancy. There is a further difficulty in that housing benefit does not cover such one-off payments, and the Exceptional Needs or Single Payments which were occasionally applied by the former Department of Health and Social Security to assist in such cases have been abolished along with the 1988 reforms to the system of social security[2].

3. *Service charges*   In addition to rent, some landlords regularly charge their tenants an amount to cover the cost of certain services which are provided in conjunction with the tenant's occupation of the accommodation. In general there are two forms of charges which a landlord can make.

The first of these affects tenants of landlords who resell electricity and gas. This is simply a question of tenants reimbursing the landlord on a periodic basis for what they consume. Ultimately however, they pay a commercial rate as opposed to a domestic rate for their gas and electricity.

Some landlords provide additional services, such as the cleaning of shared areas, communal lighting or gardening, caretaking services, or the use of an equipped kitchen in the case of groups of bedsitting flats.

The service charge made in such cases is a form of rent for the services provided.

Once again, in the case of low income households dependent upon housing benefit in particular, service charges can be a barrier to entry to such rented accommodation. This is because the housing benefit regulations stipulate that certain services provided by landlords are not eligible for consideration with the total rent payment on the basis of which housing benefit is calculated. This is true of such items as electricity, gas, and central heating. In contrast, fixed services on which a charge is payable, such as the use of a lift are generally eligible for housing benefit.

The revenue expenditure of private landlords
Landlords spend the money they have raised in revenue from their tenants on three basic areas. These are repairs and maintenance, insurance, and meeting the cost of any services they have decided to supply, and for which tenants are charged. The amount of expenditure incurred in all these areas will be influenced by the landlord's short and long term plans for the property.

1. *Maintenance and repairs* Landlords have a basic duty to carry out repairs to their property and to any fixtures and fittings, such as central heating, or sanitary fittings. Most landlords accept the need to pay attention to maintaining their property, if only to keep it in a marketable condition, so that it will continue to attract tenants and have a rent-earning capacity. If a landlord fails to carry out essential repairs, tenants can take action under the Environmental Health Acts through the local environmental health inspectorate. In cases where the tenants themselves are suspected of causing damage, the landlord may try to recover the cost of any repairs carried out from them.

2. *Insurance* Landlords will pay for insurance cover to protect both themselves and their property against a variety of risks. In the first instance, this means various disasters and hazards which might affect the building, such as floods or storms. Secondly, it also provides protection in the event of a tenant or a third party causing damage to the property. Finally, it can be set up in such a way as to protect rental income where the result of any of the first two is that the property has to be left vacant and untenanted for a period of time.

3. *Service charges* Where landlords decide to provide a specific service to their tenants, of the types referred to above, they must pay for them out of revenue, or out of the service charge income collected from tenants.

4. *Taxation*
In addition to these three areas of revenue expenditure, private landlords are taxed on their rental income. The Inland Revenue charges tax on the basis of a landlord's *actual income* from rented property during the financial year. The tax due is assessed under one of two schedules. 'Schedule A' covers mainly income from land and unfurnished property

and calculates the tax due on the basis of the landlord's net annual revenue after expenditure on management items, such as maintenance, repairs, insurance and management, has been deducted. 'Schedule D' covers furnished lettings with the additional proviso that the landlord may retain an allowance of 10% (less any occupier's rates where an inclusive rent is payable, and less any payments for services which would normally be borne by the tenant) of rents received to cover wear and tear of furniture[3].

In addition to income tax, private landlords whose turnover exceeds a figure laid down by government (currently £25,000), must be registered for VAT purposes. Until the introduction of the Community Charge, some landlords will also be responsible for the payment of rates to the local authority on their properties; others will make this the responsibility of their tenants.

Subsidised housing association activity

Because registered housing associations, in contrast to private landlords, operate with the help of public subsidies, they are very much in the public eye. In the management of their affairs they are accountable firstly to their elected management committees and the membership of the association, and thereafter to the Housing Corporation, which, as has been described in Chapter 4, has a specific role with regard to monitoring their activities.

Management committees
Management committees are elected on a regular basis, in accordance with the rules of each association. The Housing Corporation requires all associations registering with it to become registered also with the Registry of Friendly Societies, and an essential part of this registration process is the adoption of a constitution and rules. This double registration has the effect of formalising the non-profit-making status of associations, as well as obliging them to organise their membership and committee structure in accordance with the adopted rules.

Associations which do not register with the Housing Corporation, and therefore receive no Housing Corporation funds, are normally also run by committees or boards which may be either elected or appointed.

Management committees normally consist of between 7 and 15 members, though a fixed number of co-options can be made during the financial year to supplement expertise where it is felt necessary. Each year, one third of the committee membership must either stand down or submit themselves for re-election at the time of the association's annual general meeting. The committee is elected by the association's members, from which prospective candidates are drawn. Committee members come from a wide range of backgrounds — from local dignitaries, retired professionals, local politicians, community leaders, residents, and tenants.

Since the 1980 Housing Act, management committee members and their families are prevented legally from using their position to benefit financially from involvement in an association's affairs. For example, an accountant who is a member of a housing association management committee may not be paid for preparing the association's accounts; or a local resident on the committee may not, irrespective of the circumstances, be given a tenancy in association property.

Management committee control over the affairs of the association is exercised through a formal structure of meetings. The *annual general meeting (AGM)* takes place at the end of the financial year, and performs three main functions: conducting committee elections, approving the annual accounts and the annual reports by the officers of the association (the treasurer, chair, etc) on its affairs during the year, and appointing external auditors for the following year.

In addition to the AGM, there is provision for both the membership of the association and the management committee to convene *extraordinary general meetings* during the year, to discuss issues of policy. Meantime, throughout the year, on anything from a quarterly to a monthly basis, the management committee meets. From time to time, they may find it necessary to convene sub-committees or working parties to report on specific issues.

The staff of the association therefore manage the association's affairs on the committee's behalf. It is important to note however, that in spite of this apparent delegation of powers, it is the committee members who in the majority of cases are legally responsible for the financial affairs of the association. It is thus the management committee, working alongside the staff, which is responsible for determining the nature of an association's detailed management and financial objectives.

The financial objectives of housing associations

As in the case of the private rented sector, housing associations have both long and short term financial objectives. However, what has so far distinguished housing associations from the activities of private landlords is that they are prevented by virtue of their status as non-profit making bodies to engage in speculative activity. Their long-term objectives therefore are indeed about protecting their capital investment in a property, but not from the point of view of paving the way for the maximum capital gain to be made on resale. Instead, housing associations' long-term interests are about extracting the maximum social benefit over the longest period practicable.

For housing associations therefore, both their long and short term objectives focus on maintaining their property in a 'rentable' condition thus enabling it to continue to serve a useful social function. Having said this, many of the financial management decisions taken by housing associations have capital rather than revenue implications, as for example in the case of an association faced with a decision on whether it should purchase freeholds of property for which it already owns the lease, or in deciding whether to rehabilitate or modernise a particular property and the precise timing of this.

In common with private landlords, short term financial objectives are linked to the basic day-to-day management of housing, and to revenue income and expenditure. Unlike private landlords however, associations' management conduct is linked to financial constraints affecting revenue income and expenditure imposed by Government and the Housing Corporation.

Housing associations and HAG-funded activity
HAG-funded projects, in spite of reforms to HAG itself, continue as the fund centrepiece of registered housing associations. As we have said earlier, these associations cannot make a commercial profit. This means that in principle, their costs should balance with their revenue income. In reality however, many housing associations, in particular small and newly formed associations, who do not derive the same economies of scale in management enjoyed by the larger well-established associations, incur deficits. When associations run into deficit, there is provision for government to assist, by awarding revenue subsidies in cases where it is certain that the financial affairs of the association concerned are in good order, and that the deficit has not arisen as a result of some sort of malpractice. Where associations on the other hand run into surplus, there is further provision for government to claw back this surplus for redistribution to the housing association development programme as a whole.

Revenue income
1. *Rent* The Government's reforms of housing finance look forward in the future to a gradual reduction in the HAG subsidy for some housing association activity, increased use of mixed funding, the phasing out of Fair Rents for all housing association stock, and a move towards 'market' rents, previously associated only with the private rented sector. The combined effect of these changes has been to increase pressure for rent increases in a sector which has deliberately tried to keep rents within the financial means of those in need whom it set out to house.

As with private sector landlords, the major source of revenue income to housing associations is rent received. Up until April 1989, registered housing associations benefiting from HAG, and in receipt of no additional funding from the private sector, had Fair Rents registered for their properties. From April 1989, all new housing association tenancies are established as assured tenancies, and the rent payable, though broadly understood as a form of market rent, is set as an 'affordable rent'. In the same way as the private sector therefore, the two types of tenancy will coexist for a period, and Rent Officers will still be obliged to register some Fair Rents.

The Rent Officer Service applies the same criteria to registering rents in both the private rented and the housing association sector, in spite of the fact that housing associations are non-profit making, while private landlords expect profits on their activities. This means that for those continuing protected tenancies, every two years housing associations must reassess the level of rent they wish to charge, and submit their proposals to the Rent Officer who makes the final assessment, having borne in mind the views of both the housing association and the tenant. After a Fair Rent has been registered, the housing association must charge that figure to the tenant.

Housing associations are thus not obliged to charge full market rents, in the sense of this being a rent which the market can bear, other than for wholly private sector funded activity. Instead they are able to set 'affordable rents'. The point about 'affordable rents' is that they are expected to be set in relation to a housing association's actual costs of managing, maintaining and meeting debt charges on their property. At the same time, 'affordable rent' levels are expected to differ from market rent levels for the fundamental reason that in line with their original social objectives, housing associations do not seek commercial profits.

In considering future grant levels, the Housing Corporation has had to consider, in the absence of Fair Rents, how much it believes associations can reasonably charge tenants in rent. At the time of writing they have issued no detailed guidance to housing associations on how to set 'affordable rents'. Instead, the principle which it seems must be applied by associations involves deducting the costs of management, maintenance, establishing a sinking fund for cyclical maintenance, and loan repayments, from the total of the grant awarded and the amount borrowed, which will produce a shortfall in income. It is this shortfall which must then be recovered through rental income. Rent levels arrived at in this way are thus determined largely in relation to the grant levels set by the Corporation[3].

It is clear that one effect of this change is likely to be that as housing associations come to rely more on their rental income and less on government subsidies of both capital and revenue, so they will be obliged to consider carefully the ability of prospective tenants to pay rent.

2. Service charges   In addition to rent, a large number of housing associations make a service charge to tenants. This is particularly true of housing associations managing, for example, blocks of flats, sheltered housing, or hostel accommodation, where meals and the services of a resident warden might be provided, or a laundry room or communal sitting room might be included in the development.

The argument for the housing association being responsible for providing and running such services is two-fold. Firstly, certain services, such as a warden, or an emergency call system, are provided in conjunction with tenancies of dwellings because there is a perceived *need* on the part of the tenant client group for the service to be provided. This is certainly true of the services provided in sheltered housing. Secondly, in the case of services such as window cleaning or a universal heating system, there is an economic argument that where these are provided and run centrally by the association, the economies of scale reaped from the exercise can be passed on to the tenant, with the net result that they pay less.

The level of service charges set by housing associations has in the past been effectively monitored by the Fair Rent registration procedure.

Where a housing association indicated in its tenancy agreement that a service charge was payable, the Rent Officer registering a Fair Rent would also record on the certificate of Fair Rent issued for the dwelling, this fact. Furthermore, when an association made its initial application for a Fair Rent to be registered, it had to provide a list of the services it provided in conjunction with the tenancy, along with details of the sum of money contained within the service charge which was attributable to each particular service. The system of 'market' or 'affordable' rents has no formal administrative procedures of this type. This means that associations are required to outline any commitment they wish to make about the provision of services in the assured tenancy agreement, which then forms the basis of a contract between landlord and tenant. It is then up to individual associations to decide how to make details of expenditure on services available to tenants.

Revenue expenditure
Under the pre-1989 system of HAG, a housing association's revenue income was important in that it was taken into account when HAG was being calculated, and it was from this income that loan repayments to the Housing Corporation had to be found in future years. Under the new system, by making housing associations responsible for setting their own rent levels, they also become responsible for any revenue deficits which might be incurred. For these reasons, housing associations have always had as one of their principal objectives the maximisation of their rental income. They pursue this by monitoring and improving management, by dealing with tenancy matters promptly, by controlling voids, tackling arrears, and planning maintenance.

The main areas of revenue expenditure in housing associations fall into the same categories as those described in relation to the private rented sector. Associations incur expenditure on the management and maintenance of their properties, including staffing and office costs. However, the amount of money which a housing association is permitted to spend on management and maintenance is tied to set *management and maintenance allowances*. These are laid down and reassessed regularly by the Housing Corporation, and are based on a sum of permitted expenditure for each dwelling under management. Housing associations are expected to remain within these spending limits. Management and maintenance allowances thus form the basis of a housing association's annual revenue budget, as it is possible to calculate from the allowances exactly how much money the association is permitted to spend in the forthcoming year.

Now and again unforeseen major items of revenue expenditure, such as an unexpected major repair, or additional staff costs caused by absence, mean that housing associations sometimes exceed these limits on expenditure. In the case of large repair items, it may be possible to avoid this situation by treating the work — say, a roof replacement — as a capital repair. In the past, where the capital costs of such a project had originally been funded through HAG, housing associations could apply to the Housing Corporation for additional HAG to fund capital repairs of this kind. From 1989, HAG for capital repairs has been abolished. This means that housing associations themselves are now wholly responsible for meeting the cost of major repairs, and are expected to set up sinking funds to manage these costs effectively. The cost of making payments to the sinking fund then counts as management and maintenance expenditure.

Revenue subsidies
The main form of revenue subsidy for which housing associations can be considered is Revenue Deficit Grant. It is expected that in the medium term this subsidy will gradually be phased out.

The principle of Revenue Deficit Grant (RDG) has been that when an association's revenue account is in deficit at the end of the financial year for reasons other than those mentioned above, it can apply to the Housing Corporation for a revenue subsidy. The object of RDG has been that it make good revenue deficits where it is clear from the application submitted and from the accounts, that the association has managed its affairs during the preceding year in such a way that it has maximised its revenue through good management practice, but that in spite of this, a deficit has been incurred. In the case of housing association schemes funded through local authorities, it has been possible for the local authority concerned to make a Rate Fund Contribution for similar reasons.

In line with this principle therefore, an association which has allowed a high level of voids to develop would be unlikely to be considered for RDG, unless there was good reason for the voids occurring, say, if the dwellings concerned had had to be vacated to allow repairs to be carried out. Small or developing associations have been more reliant upon RDG, as the deficits they incur are seen as a consequence of management and maintenance allowances being insufficient to cover the full actual costs of providing the minimum basic staff support they require. The point here is that small associations' staffing costs in particular are relatively high compared to larger associations.

Where an association has incurred a revenue deficit and is considered ineligible for RDG, it is expected to make adjustments in its own organisation and finances. The short-term effect is that the burden of any expenditure on capital repairs, or of a deficit or overspend, will be carried through to the following accounting year, when it will impact on that year's revenue budget. In some cases, financial problems of this type have resulted in associations being instructed by the Housing Corporation to sell property to make good the deficit.

One of the original justifications for RDG was that since rents registered under the Fair Rent system for many years were not rising in line with inflation, the rental income of associations was kept artificially low, and needed to be 'topped up' to allow them to continue to function. More recently, rents have begun to rise, and the introduction of 'affordable' rents should in theory allow associations to collect rents which tenants can afford on the one hand, and which meet revenue expenditure on the other. As a result of this rising rental income, the Housing Corporation predicts that within a few years there will be no or little requirement for revenue subsidies like RDG.

Rent Surplus Fund (Grant Redemption Fund)
Having discussed the situation with regard to shortfalls in housing association revenue income, it is important to note that some of the larger long-established housing associations have now paid off the capital loans on some of their projects, and are generating surpluses from continued rental income. More and more housing association projects over time will inevitably move into surplus. Aware that this would happen, the Government under the 1980 Housing Act introduced Grant Redemption Fund (GRF) as a mechanism for clawing back some of these funds for reinvestment. The scheme became fully operational in 1983.

The principle behind GRF has been that where a registered housing association which has received HAG in the past moves into surplus in its revenue account, that surplus must be transferred into the central fund. This requires associations to organise their housing stock into class types which reflect the type of subsidy paid, as follows:

Class A rent accommodation
Class B shared-ownership accommodation
Class C hostel accommodation
Class D co-ownership, community leasehold and short-life
Class E almshouses

Net rental income is then calculated for each class of stock owned by the association: this is the figure which remains after specified deductions have been made for management and maintenance, loan charges, and service provision. The net rental income is deemed to represent the actual surplus accruing to the association.

Once the surplus has been calculated, before the funds are permanently clawed back, a check is made on whether a proportion of the surplus can be applied to make good any existing revenue deficits being carried by the association. Thereafter at the end of the financial year, the funds due to GRF, after deficits have been met, are paid to the DoE. The total GRF collected by the DoE is then reinvested in the Housing Corporation's Gross ADP in the following year.

From April 1989, the Fund has been known as the Rental Surplus Fund. Associations will be allowed to retain around 70% of any surpluses generated for the express functions of building up reserves and establishing sinking funds to help meet the future costs of any capital repairs.

It is important to note that housing association projects funded through mixed funding arrangements may not make claims on RDG, and at the same time nor are they obliged to return surpluses to the Rental Surplus Fund.

Control: The Property Revenue Account
The Property Revenue Account, which associations are required to maintain and submit to the Housing Corporation at the end of

the financial year, records all the revenue income and expenditure transactions referred to above, in respect of the entire stock of an individual housing association. Where an association manages a number of different types of scheme, such as Fair Rent or assured tenancies, shared ownership or hostels, each scheme type must have a separate account.

The Property Revenue Account shows whether a deficit or a surplus has been incurred. In the case of the latter, it goes on to show the amount of money transferred to GRF. The net deficit or surplus remaining after this transfer has been made, is then transferred into the General Income and Expenditure Account, which, after linking this to the development functions, and so the capital transactions of the association, is combined to produce a picture of the entire financial position.

The new regime: housing association activity generated using private funds

Throughout this chapter we have made a number of references to changes to the framework of housing association finance, to the way in which capital funding is to be provided by the private sector, and also to the way in which rental income is to be raised in future. At present, housing association activity generated using private finance falls into three main categories. Firstly, there is mixed funding activity, which continues to receive a reduced HAG subsidy from the Housing Corporation, and which is therefore undertaken by registered housing associations. In addition to this category, some registered housing associations have become interested in providing housing using private finance alone. In order to do this, for legal reasons associated with the non-profit making status of registered housing associations, they must set up a separate unregistered association. Finally, there is a large number of existing unregistered housing associations, whose aim has always been to provide privately funded housing. What all of these activities have in common is that they charge market rents to their tenants. However, all three types of project are associated with different levels of loan charges, all of which must be met by revenue income.

The implications of such activity for revenue income and expenditure are twofold. Firstly, even in the case of those associations receiving subsidy in the form of reduced fixed HAG under mixed funding rules, the total revenue income requirement — the sum of money needed to meet the costs of running the business, maintaining the property and meeting the loan repayments — must be raised from rents. Projects of this type do not qualify for any further Government subsidy on either capital or revenue. These factors taken together determine the financial objectives of associations running such schemes, which require to raise rents to meet higher revenue costs and provide a cushion for the risks *they* rather than the Housing Corporation bear.

The second consideration therefore involves the phasing out of Fair Rents and introduction of assured tenancies into the housing association sector, as required by the 1988 Housing Act. This will clearly assist associations working in this area of activity, strengthening their ability to increase rental income to meet increased costs.

At the same time as these measures have been introduced, there is still a desire amongst the policy makers to emphasise the remaining fundamental difference between the traditional property interests of private landlords and housing associations, with the requirement that housing associations using HAG — either on its own or in conjunction with private funding — charge 'affordable rents', as opposed to the 'market rents' charged by private landlords and some unsubsidised associations.

Conclusion

In this chapter we have sought to identify the financial objectives which underlie the management of rented housing in the independent sector and which affect the way in which revenue is raised and how it is spent.

In the case of the private landlord, there is a wide degree of freedom in defining these objectives, with the long term objectives, which relate to the future of the building as a capital investment, effectively fixing the context for the definition of the short-term objectives. Though there are some controls for certain categories of private sector tenancy which restrict rents and so restrict revenue income, in practice it is a fairly simple matter for landlords to decide upon which restrictions they are willing to accept.

In the case of housing associations, the financial objectives are to a large extent defined broadly by government which has an interest in ensuring that its capital investment is being looked after. Once again these longer term concerns fix the context for the shorter term ones. In practice, the short-term objectives have also been overseen by government which, for example, sets parameters for deficit funding applications, and provides for 'claw-back' of surpluses where they accrue.

Mixed funding housing association initiatives are beginning to bridge the gap. In return for becoming more independent financially of government, the Government is withdrawing from its role as scrutineer of the affair of housing associations pursuing such initiatives by abolishing rent controls, withdrawing RDG and GRF, and encouraging the generation of surpluses by leaving them intact for associations to reinvest themselves. Housing association activity is as a result becoming more closely identified in the eyes of the consumer with the private sector.

The 1988 Housing Act has lifted rent controls and paved the way for the expansion of assured tenancies and introduction of market rents in both the private rented sector and the housing association sector. For the consumer, this new 'independent rented sector' as a whole can now be split into a number of new sub-sectors, distinguishable no longer in terms of the particular rent regime which governs them, but rather in terms of the source of their capital finance, which in turn determines the rent and therefore the price of gaining entry. For the low income consumer, success in securing a tenancy from a private landlord or an unregistered housing association in particular will depend largely upon the capacity of housing benefit to cover the costs of the new higher market rents which must inevitably be charged.

Notes

1 See for example *Roof*, September/October 1986, November/December 1986, and July/August 1987.
2 The 1988 Social Security Act.
3 See Treanor, Dave, 'After the Act – setting rents', in *Housing Association Weekly*, 4 November 1988, for discussion of the nature of the decisions facing associations when considering rent setting policies.

Chapter 8
Running costs of local authority housing services

Introduction

Chapter 5 describes the housing services provided by local authorities within the content of local authority services as a whole, the distinction between capital and revenue expenditure and the local government practice of fund accounting. It also describes the way local authorities raise the money to pay for capital assets and the controls the Government places on such activities. This chapter completes the description of the financing of local authority housing services by describing how local authorities raise money to pay for the running expenses of the housing services and how the Government controls and influences such expenditure.

In Chapter 5 the finance of capital expenditure was considered in the context of the 'Housing Plan.' The planning process required the members and officers of the local authority to define objectives for the housing services and produce a budget of schemes that would achieve these objectives within the financial constraints under which the authority is operating. The capital programme will be implemented to build and improve council houses and also to offer grants and loans to private sector tenants. Most of this capital expenditure will generate a commitment to pay annual running costs. Houses for rent will need to be managed and the local authority will need to employ administrators, accountants and rent collectors. Older houses will need repair and maintenance, this means spending money on materials and craftsmen's wages. The local authority will borrow money to finance grants and loans to the private sector and this money will need to be repaid with interest. These running costs fall partly on council tenants, who contribute by paying rent, partly by the national taxpayers, through a system of government grants paid to the housing authority, and partly on the local taxpayer. A major constraint on the 'Housing Plan' must be the extent to which tenants and taxpayers can afford to pay for the capital schemes needed to achieve the housing objectives.

Chapter 5 also dealt with old (pre-1990) and new (post-1990) financial regimes. Moreover 1990 sees the introduction of new systems of funding and control from revenue spending, and these will be discussed in this chapter.

Revenue finance budgeting

Capital budgeting deals with planning and implementing capital schemes. Such budgets are usually prepared as rolling programmes and include not only detailed permission to spend for the current year, but also planned spending for, say, the next three years. Revenue budgets deal with planning and implementing revenue schemes, that is the running costs of the service. Revenue budgets are usually produced for one year at a time and provide detailed plans of, and permissions to spend on, running costs. In preparing the revenue budget the housing authority will again be required to state its objectives for the housing service and to try and achieve them within the funds available to it.

Housing authorities are engaged in providing three quite separate services. The first, the Housing Benefit system gives help to all tenants on low incomes by reducing the payments they have to make through local taxation and rents. The money to pay Housing Benefits comes from the local and national taxpayers. The second activity is the provision of council housing, this will be paid for by tenants and local and national taxpayers until April 1990, after which the contribution from local taxpayers will cease. The third activity is giving assistance through loans and grants to private sector tenants and this is paid for by local and national taxpayers.

Assistance available to all tenants

Housing authorities are responsible for administering the Housing Benefits scheme. This delivers means tested help with the payment of rent and local taxation. The impact on the housing service of the Housing Benefit system is limited to the benefits available to reduce rent. Assistance to eligible council tenants takes the form of rent rebates which reduce the liability to pay rent bills. Eligible private sector tenants receive rent allowances which are cash payments to help pay rent to their landlords. Local authorities are required to operate standard schemes for rebates and allowances but may operate more generous schemes if they so wish. Most of the cost (over 90%) of operating the standard scheme is met by central government grant and the residual cost, including the extra cost of running a more generous scheme, is met by the local authority from general funds.

Housing Benefits are part of the network of income support grants paid to individuals by central government; the role of the local authorities in the scheme is mainly administrative. While most central government spending is 'cash limited', i.e. annual spending on a service must be contained within a stated amount, Housing Benefit expenditure is considered to be 'demand led' and the government will pay whatever is necessary to meet the claims allowed. This means that the local authority must also treat its contribution to tenants as 'demand led' and, if necessary, reduce its other spending to pay for increased demand for rent rebates and allowances.

The provision of council housing

The running costs of providing council houses and the funds to pay for it are kept in a separate fund called the Housing Revenue Account (HRA). All the expenses of running the council house service are charged to the HRA and the Council must ensure that sufficient funds are paid into the account to meet service expenses.

The 'old' regime
In the 1980s housing authorities were required to set 'reasonable rents'. At the same time the authority was required to 'balance' its Housing Revenue Account by ensuring that spending matched funds available. The main funds available were rents, government grants and interest on investments. If the income from these sources exceeded expenditure then the surplus could either be carried forward to help pay for next year's spending or transferred to the general fund. If these funds did not cover the cost of running the service then the local authority had to make up the deficit from general funds.

Under this system a local authority could choose one of four options
   (a) require council tenants to pay the net cost of the service; or
   (b) charge lower rents than in (a) and charge the shortfall to the local taxpayer; or
   (c) charge higher rents than in (a) and use the surplus for council house spending in other years; or
   (d) charge rents as in (c) but transfer the surplus to the general fund to pay for services provided for the local taxpayer.
A council that chose (a) would require its local taxpayers to subsidise services to tenants, while a council that chose (d) would require its tenants to subsidise its local taxpayers.

A flavour of the different financing strategies used by housing authorities under the 'old' regime can be found in the following examples which are taken from statistics published by the Chartered Institute of Public Finance and Accountancy showing estimated funding for 1989/90:

Authority A   Net expenditure to be charged to tenants and taxpayers of £25mn and housing support subsidy of £7.3mn. Decides to finance £1.2mn from balances and charge the rest to tenants at an average rent of £35 per dwelling per week.

Authority B   Net expenditure to be charged to tenants and taxpayers of £45,5mn, no housing support subsidy. Decides to charge 92% of cost to tenants at an average rent of £17.50 per dwelling per week and charge the rest to the general funds of the authority.

Authority C   Net expenditure to be charged to tenants and taxpayers of £2.3mn and negligible housing support subsidy. Decides to charge over full cost to tenants with average rents of £16 per dwelling per week and make a contribution to general funds of £1.8mn.

Spending on council housing

The annual budget is used not only to direct permission to spend but also to set the rent levels for the coming year. Details of annual budgets are collected and published by the Chartered Institute of Public Finance and Accountancy and their 'Housing Revenue Account Statistics 1989-90 Estimates' are a useful guide to the financing of council housing in the last year of the old grant regime.

The expected spending in England and Wales for 1989/90 can be seen in Figure 3.8.1.

	£'000	%
Expenditure		
Supervision and Management	1,398,556	21
Repairs and maintenance	1,930,853	29
Cost of capital	3,262,393	48
Other expenses	165,102	2
	6,756,904	100

Figure 3.8.1

Source: CIPFA HRA statistics 1989/90

Looking at the three major headings in turn:

Management and supervision
On average housing authorities spend about £200 per council dwelling per year on supervision and management expenses with some authorities spending considerably more than this. This spending pays for the provision of 'general' services to all tenants such as rent collecting and accounting, and on 'special services' to some tenants such as caretaking and cleaning services provided for the elderly or disabled.

Once the basic service to the tenant has been established the authority will probably be happy to handle future development on an incremental basis, making changes as and when they are required rather than reassessing the basic provision each year. Once the level of service to be provided in 1989/90 was decided each authority probably used the cost of supervision and management in 1988/89 as a starting point for the budget, adjusting this figure for changes required to service level provisions and inflation to arrive at the budget for 1989/90.

Cost of repair and maintenance
As landlords, local authorities have a statutory duty to 'keep in repair and proper working order' the structure and exterior, and the internal installations for services, sanitation and space heating or heating water of the houses they offer for rent. Local authorities can undertake commitments beyond the minimum prescribed by statute, if they wish.

The duty to repair and maintain houses goes beyond mere legal form, the local authority holds the houses in trust for future generations of tenants and it can be argued that the councillors have a moral duty to ensure that the housing stock does not deteriorate for lack of proper repair and maintenance.

In 1989/90 authorities plan to spend £2,845mn on repair and maintenance, financing £1,931mn by direct charges to the Housing Revenue Accounts and a further £914mn from capital.

In preparing the budget for 1989/90 for 'repair and maintenance' authorities will need to establish how much work needs to be done. They may well approach this problem by considering schemes in two categories, that which can be planned, such as rewiring the dwellings on part of a council estate, and those where the authority is required to respond to requests from the tenants. The authority must then decide how much it is prepared to spend on repairs and maintenance in the year and how this will be financed.

Cost of raising funds for the capital programme
In Chapter 5 the financing of capital expenditure was described and the sources of finance were identified as current income, borrowing, leasing and capital receipts. If the expenditure is to acquire or improve council houses then there may be a charge to the housing revenue account.

Using capital receipts or current income to finance capital expenditure have one thing in common, the cost of the asset is charged to the fund in the year of purchase. Hence an asset financed from capital receipts would be charged to the fund holding capital receipts in the year of purchase while an asset funded from current council house income would be charged to the Housing Revenue Account in the year of purchase.

While financing from current income and capital receipts have an impact on only one year's funds, leasing and borrowing will affect more than one year. If an asset is acquired for council house purposes through a lease it will normally be paid for over a number of years and each payment will be met annually from the Housing Revenue Account. If the asset is financed from loan, that is the housing service borrows money through the Consolidated Loans Fund (see Chapter 5), the Housing Revenue Account will be required to pay an annual charge covering repayment of the loan with interest to the CLF until the loan is repaid.

Of the £3,262mn likely charge to Housing Revenue Accounts in 1989/90 £93mn will be spent on capital schemes charged directly to the current funds, £490mn will be used to repay outstanding debt and the remaining £2,678mn will be spent on paying interest.

In budgeting for the cost of debt repayment in 1989/90 the authority is likely to use to the debt outstanding at the end of 1989 as a starting point, adjusting the figure for new loans to be raised and old loans repaid in 1989/90. The authority will also need to make provision for interest payments and for this they will need to forecast interest rates, a notoriously difficult task.

Net cost of the council house service as borne by tenants and taxpayers

Not all the costs of the council house service fall on tenants and taxpayers, the service is allowed to use interest from the investment of unspent capital receipts to meet expenditure and to charge separately for some services provided eg rent of garages.

In 1989/90 these sources of income are expected to reduce the impact on charges to tenants and taxpayers by the amounts shown in Figure 3.8.2.

	£'000	£'000
Expenditure as above		6,756,904
less:		
Interest on investments	958,091	
Other income	399,881	
	————	1,357,972
		—————
		5,398,932
		—————

Figure 3.8.2

Source: CIPFA HRA statistics 1989/90

Interest on investments
In the 1980s the sale of council houses raised over £12.5 billion. Some of this money was reinvested in the housing service but a substantial proportion was not. Monies not reinvested in the housing service were invested elsewhere and the interest earned treated as income to the HRA.

The HRA also earned income through the interest payments from ex-tenants given mortgages to allow them to implement their 'right to buy'.

In estimating the amount of interest likely to be earned in 1989/90 the authorities would be required to guess not only the future rate of interest but also the sales of council houses during 1989/90 and the extent to which they would apply these.

Use of 'balances'
If a Housing Revenue Account is in surplus that surplus can be carried forward into the next year to help pay for future council house spending. Housing authorities estimated that at 1 April 1989 they would have £463,258,000 to carry forward into future years and plan to use £127,102,000 of this in 1989/90. Figure 3.8.3 shows how this will further reduce the charge to tenants and taxpayers.

	£'000
Expenditure as above	5,398,932
less	
use of balances	127,102
Net cost borne by tenant and taxpayer	5,271,830

Figure 3.8.3
Source: CIPFA HRA statistics 1989/90

The amounts raised from rents, government subsidy to the housing service and deficit contributions from the general funds of the housing authorities were expectd to be £5,443,547 with the surplus collected being transferred to general funds as shown in Figure 3.8.4.

	£'000
Gross rents	4,763,461
Housing Support Subsidy	374,510
General Fund	305,576
	5,443,547
less net expenditure	5,271,830
Surplus transferred to General Fund	171,717

Figure 3.8.4
Source: CIPFA HRA statistics 1989/90

Gross rents
When a housing authority accepts a tenant the two parties agree on the weekly amount of rent to be paid. This will not always be the same as the amount paid by the tenant to the rent collector. Before 1990 the amount collected would have included an element for rates and would, for some tenants, be reduced by the amount of housing benefit payable. The accounting system would ensure that the HRA would be given the credit for the agreed or 'gross rent' payable rather than the payment

made by the tenant. In 1989/90 about 48% of council house gross rents were expected to be paid through housing benefits.

In budgeting for cash raised from rents the authority would be influenced by tenants' ability to pay. Although in theory low-income groups should be able, with help from the housing benefits grants, to pay their rent many could argue that even with such assistance not everyone could afford a rent increase. The level of rent must be set so that the planned cash budget is met with the minimum of 'forced' bad debts.

Housing Support Subsidy
When the Housing Support Subsidy was introduced in 1980 it signalled a radical change in the way the Government was prepared to help pay for the cost of council housing. Previous grants had come in various different guises but were mainly linked to the cost of borrowing so that any housing authority that was building new houses was assured of getting some grant from the government to help with running costs. The Housing Support Subsidy was different and was designed to help those authorities most in need of help and to encourage efficiency in the provision of council housing. For the first time the grant was calculated in such a way that even authorities with a building programme could be assessed as unworthy of grant.

The following formula was used to calculate the grant payable to the authority in the year of account:

Base figure
+
element for inflation plus 'real' growth
−
recommended rent increases

The base figure for each year was the grant paid in the previous year (in 1981/82 this would have been the grant paid in 1980/81 when all housing authorities received grant under the previous grant regime), the element for inflation and recommended rent increases to be calculated using national guidelines set by the Government and all figures adjusted for movements in housing stock levels.

For example the Government's expenditure plans published in January 1988 proposed a guideline rent increase of £1.60 per week per council dwelling and a guideline 9.2% increase in management and maintenance allowance as a basis for grant settlement. These guidelines applied to all housing authorities in England and Wales and were used by the Government not only for the purpose of grant calculation but also to advise housing authorities as to good practice. But the housing authorities were not required to put these guidelines into practice, they could choose to budget for higher price and volume increases in service provision while keeping rents down, increased deficits being met from increased contributions from general funds.

Thus the Government assessed each authority's need for grant on the basis of a 'notional' Housing Revenue Account that it produced itself, an account that might bear little resemblance to the Housing Revenue Account kept by the local authority.

When the formula for the grant calculation was applied to individual local authorities it could produce one of three answers. If the answer was positive then the authority received the amount calculated in grant, if the answer was zero, or negative, then no grant was payable. By 1986/87 only 24% of housing authorities in England and Wales were still receiving Housing Support Subsidy.

General funds
The extent to which the authority is prepared to use general funds to meet housing costs and vice versa will depend on the level of available funds and what can be spared for housing purposes.

Comparison of the 1980/81 Housing Revenue Account totals for all authorities in England and Wales with the equivalent estimated figures for 1989/90 as shown in Figure 3.8.5 gives an indication of the effect the regimes for capital spending and rent levels introduced in April 1981 had on the expenditure and funding for council housing.

Local authority HRA
Structure of income and expenditure
England and Wales

	1980/81 Actual %	1989/90 Estimated %
Expenditure		
Supervision and management	13	20
Repair and maintenance	20	28
Cost of capital	63	48
Other expenditure	6	2
Transfers to general fund	0	2
	100	100
Income		
Rents paid by tenants	37	33
Rent rebates	8	36
Housing support subsidy	32	5
Interest	4	14
Other income	6	6
Transfers from general fund	13	4
Use of balances	0	2
	100	100

Figure 3.8.5

Source: CIPFA HRA statistics 1980/81 and Housing Finance by B. Bucknell

These statistics show:

   (a) Cost of capital as a proportion of total expenditure has fallen from 63% to 48%. In 1980 the Government introduced the HIP allocation system to control council house capital spending and each year the allocations for housing purposes became less generous.

   (b) In 1980/81 gross rents met 45% of the cost of council housing, in 1989/90 69%. Meanwhile housing support subsidy contributed 32% in 1980/81 and a mere 5% in 1989/90. This shift of the burden of financing away from government subsidy of the housing service towards higher rent contributions reflects Government policy of targeting funds towards those authorities most in need of financial support. The Housing Support Subsidy directed funds towards authorities most in need of help while influencing authorities that were better off to raise rents to match raised expenditure.

   (c) The Government also wished to target the funds at its disposal towards individuals in need. Any subsidy payable to a housing authority would be used to reduce general rent levels, reduction of individual rent bills was to be achieved through the housing benefit system. In theory local authorities could raise general rent levels secure in the knowledge that tenants on low incomes would be protected from such rises by increased housing benefits. In 1980/81 rent rebates paid for 8% of the cost of the service and in 1989/90 36%. During the period 1980/81 to 1989/90 average weekly rents rose from £11.61 to £20.85.

The likely impact of new legislation on the Housing Revenue Account

It is likely that, superficially, post-1990 Housing Revenue Accounts will look rather like those of the 1980s. Expenditure will still include the costs of supervision and management, repairs and maintenance and the cost of capital, and income will still include gross rents and housing subsidy but there will be one major difference, the housing authority will no longer be allowed to subsidise rents from the general funds of the authority. It is also likely that the total spent on housing, the proportions spent on the different expenditure heads and the level of rents paid by tenants could alter significantly.

The legislation that will affect the Housing Revenue Accounts is the 'right to choose' allowed to tenants under the Housing Act 1988 and the new capital controls and 'ringfencing' of council house expenditure introduced in the Local Government and Housing Act of 1989.

'The right to choose'
The Government is committed to encouraging a housing market where local authorities are 'enablers' rather than providers of housing. Tenants already have the 'right to buy' (see Chapter 5); the Housing Act 1988 gives them the 'right to choose' a landlord. If the new landlord can raise

the necessary funds, persuade the majority of tenants asked to choose him, and prove acceptable to the Housing Corporation, he can require the local authority to sell him the houses he wants.

The Housing Revenue Account records spending on council housing. If the council builds or buys more dwellings then it is likely that spending and income will go up, conversely if they sell or otherwise lose dwellings then spending and income should drop. However it does not follow that if 1% of dwellings are sold that all expenditure and income figures will drop by 1%. This is partly because the 1% sold may not generate 1% of cost and rent but also because some types of income and expenditure are more responsive to small changes in the level of housing stock held than others; for instance the sale of one house will result in a loss of rent income but may have a negligible effect on the costs of supervision and management. The changes in council house costs and income for individual authorities will depend on the scale of disposals and the costs and income associated with the properties that are sold. Some authorities are planning to dispose of all their council houses thus keeping a HRA in name only.

The controls on capital expenditure

The changes proposed in the Local Government and Housing Act 1989 may have a considerable impact on the scale of charges to the Housing Revenue Accounts for repair and maintenance and the cost of capital. The old and new systems are described and assessed in Chapter 5, this chapter will concentrate on the extent to which the new system will affect the levels of spending on council house running costs.

The decapitalisation of 'repairs and maintenance'

In 1986 the Audit Commission published 'Improving Council House Maintenance' which concluded that many council houses were not being properly maintained despite councils being allowed access to loans and sale proceeds. The significance of this, from a financing point of view was that:

— the definition of works for which local authorities could borrow long term funds was more generous than generally accepted accounting theory would permit;
— despite this, local authority housing was, in some instances, inadequately maintained and repaired; and
— some local authorities were reluctant to raise rents to levels at which they would have sufficient funds to properly maintain the housing stock.

The Local Government and Housing Act introduces a new definition of works that can be capitalised which does not include 'repair and maintenance' and from 1 April 1990 housing authorities will not be able to reduce the impact of their repairs programme on the Housing Revenue Account by the use of loans or capital receipts. This change will have little effect on housing authorities with well maintained stock and a policy of charging repairs and maintenance to revenue, but for those authorities with poorly maintained stock who rely heavily on the permission to borrow to finance 'repairs and maintenance' this could present grave problems. Such authorities would be forced to either increase the level of revenue spending on repairs and maintenance or allow the housing stock for which they are responsible to deteriorate further.

Debt repayment and the 'cost of capital'

In most Housing Revenue Accounts the major spending on 'cost of capital' is associated with the repayment of debt. Before 1990 local authorities were required to repay the debt on an asset within a 'loan sanction period' prescribed by the government; this period was approximately equivalent to the life of the asset. The authority was also allowed to repay the loans from capital receipts if they wished to.

Proposals in the Local Government and Housing Act require that from 1 April 1990:

— a proportion of capital receipts should be set aside for the repayment of debt or meeting other credit liabilities. The proportion proposed for housing receipts is 75% (50% for other receipts), but this can be varied by the Secretary of State, and

— the Secretary of State requires the debt repayment from the Housing Revenue Account should be at least equal to

$$\text{the balance of debt outstanding at the beginning of the year} \times \text{a rate prescribed by the Secretary of State}$$

The rate to be applied can be varied by the Secretary of State and he may order different rates for different authorities and services.

In recent years the debt repayment charge to the Housing Revenue Account has increased annually as new borrowing is made to finance capital expenditure. The requirement that all local authorities should use 75% of their housing capital receipts to reduce debt repayment, either directly by repayment of old debt or indirectly by using capital receipts instead of loans to finance new capital spending will slow down the rate of increase of debt repayment, perhaps even to the extent of turning the annual increase into an annual reduction.

The second proposal, that local authorities repay a required minimum of their debt each year gives the Secretary of State control over the size of local authority debt, both for individual authorities and for authorities as a whole.

The likely effect of this legislation is that in the near future some housing authorities, those with relatively low outstanding debts and relatively high sales proceeds, will become debt free.

It is also likely that the requirement that at least 75% of capital receipts be used in the year in which they are earned will mean that authorities will no longer hold large balances of capital receipts earning interest that can be treated as income to the Housing Revenue Account.

'Ringfencing' the Housing Revenue Account
On 27 July 1988 the Department of the Environment published a consultation paper entitled 'New Financial Regime for Local Authority Housing in England and Wales', in which the old regime of financing council house running costs was criticised and a new regime proposed.

Among the criticisms of the 'old' regime were:
— there were anomalies in funding, for example in 1987/88 24 authorities that received Housing Support Subsidy made contributions from their HRAs to general funds. This indicated that the Housing Support Subsidy formula was failing to distribute the total subsidy available to those authorities most in need of assistance;
— by 1987/88 three-quarters of authorities were not receiving subsidy towards the cost of repairs and maintenance and this could be a financial incentive to depress maintenance spending below the guidelines; and
— local authorities were not sending direct signals to tenants through rent levels. Increased expenditure on the service could be met from general funds rather than rent increases. The Government considered that this would allow inefficient local authorities to hide the extra costs due to inefficiency from the tenants.

The Government's objectives for the new regime were that it would:
— be simpler and more easily understood;
— be fairer to tenants and local taxpayers, delivering rents which were within the reach of people in low paid employment and linked to what the property is worth; and
— should direct the subsidy to where it was most needed, providing an incentive for good management rather than a cover for bad practice and inefficiency.

The 'new regime' will be introduced from 1 April 1990 under the powers contained in the Local Government and Housing Act 1989.

From 1 April 1990 housing authorities lose the right to make discretionary transfers from general funds to subsidise council house rent levels. The net expenditure on the service must be financed from government subsidy and rents. This separation of the funding for running the council house service is often referred to as 'ringfencing', implying that the service is now divorced from the general financing of the authority. This is not the case as in practice the ringfence only stops general funds going into the housing revenue account. Housing authorities will still be allowed to make discretionary transfers from council house funds to the general funds of the authority, but only if the authority is not receiving housing subsidy.

A critical element in the new regime is the new system for distributing the central government subsidy. This new subsidy is intended to replace the existing housing support subsidy, the rent rebate subsidy and the transfer made by housing authorities from general funds and is calculated in two parts:

— an element to meet the Government's share of housing benefits allowed to tenants. This is calculated in a similar way to the current grant and is aimed at ensuring that income support goes to needy individuals; and

— an element similar to the old housing support subsidy which will target funds to authorities most in need of support.

The grant is intended to make good the deficit which would arise in the Housing Revenue Account if the housing was managed with 'reasonable efficiency' and the deficit for each authority will be calculated by reference to a 'notional' Housing Revenue Account in which the Government uses its own guideline figures to calculate the impact of inflation and recommended rent rises.

There are two major differences between the old housing support grant and the new Housing Revenue Account grant:

— the legislation provides that the guideline rent increases will be issued on a local rather than national basis. The Government will issue guideline rents for each authority assessed by comparing the gross sales prices on 'right to buy' sales in the authority's area with similar figures for other housing authorities. The recommended increase in rents for the year will be the difference between the Government's assessed rents and the current actual rent levels in the authority. The Government recognises that it may be asking local authorities to make substantial rent increases in the first few years of the new grant regimes and therefore is prepared to 'damp' the impact of the changes by defining an 'acceptable limit' to the increase. For example in 1990/91 the rent increases guidelines proposed for England would not exceed £4.50 per dwelling per week. This damping mechanism may become a permanent feature of the system; and

— what happens when the grant calculation returns a negative answer. From 1990/91, if the 'notional' HRA is in deficit, then the authority will be paid grant equal to the deficit.

If the 'notional' HRA produces a surplus then the authority will be required to transfer an amount equal to that surplus from the Housing Revenue Account to another fund of the authority.

The following illustrations show how the new grant regime could work for three authorities.

Example 1   An authority with a Rent Rebate Grant assessed at £3mn and a 'notional' Housing Revenue Account deficit of £1.5mn will receive £4.5mn funds into the Housing Revenue Account.

Example 2   An authority with a Rent Rebate Grant assessed at £4.2mn and a 'notional' Housing Revenue Account surplus of £1.2mn will receive funds of £4.2mn into the Housing Revenue Account and lose funds of £1.2mn giving a net increase in funds of £3mn.

Example 3   An authority with a Rent Rebate Grant assessed at £2.5mn and a 'notional' Housing Revenue Account surplus of £3.5mn will receive funds of £2.5mn into the Housing Revenue Account and lose funds of £3.5mn giving a net decrease in funds of £1.0mn.

The Government expects that in time all Housing Revenue Accounts will be self-financing rather than dependent on funding from the national taxpayer.

The major impact of 'ringfencing' on the HRA budgeting procedure is that rent levels will have to be set to balance the account without any help from general funds.

Criticisms of the HRA not addressed by the Government in the new legislation

HRA's are designed to show the bills paid to run the council house service and how the money to pay those bills was collected. They are also used for other purposes than this:

As a source of information for the planning process
The HRA records the money paid by housing authorities to provide the council house service and the income raised to finance this expenditure. The information contained in the HRA is used for planning purposes. The housing authority will use the information to adjust their rent levels in line with the cost of provision. The government will use notional figures, partly based on actuals, to determine the levels of grants payable to local authorities. It is therefore important to establish whether the HRA produces figures that reflect the cost of providing council houses. Many argue that the HRA fails to do this in a satisfactory way. The arguments offered are that some expenditure currently in the HRA is not housing expenditure and should not be used in determining rent and grant levels, conversely some costs not included in the HRA should be included for rent and grant setting purposes.

Expenditure that is in the HRA and, it is argued, should be discounted for planning purposes arises when a local authority, pays more for an asset than its 'housing worth'. For example an authority which buys land by compulsory purchase in an inner city area might have to pay more than market value for the land. The price paid under compulsory purchase is fixed according to statutory regulations and may exceed the price a developer would be prepared to pay for a site requiring expensive clearance and preparation. The extra cost filters through to the HRA via the debt charges paid on the loan raised to buy the land.

Expenditure not in the HRA but which, it is argued, should be included for planning purposes, includes adequate liability to repair the housing stock and an element for the replacement costs of the housing stock. It is widely accepted that many council houses are in need of repair and maintenance and it can be argued therefore that the level of expenditure on repairs and maintenance in the national aggregate HRA is inadequate and should not be used as an indicator of the future need to spend or as a base for setting rents.

As an indicator of the extent to which council house rent is subsidised
It is argued that the true subsidy given to tenants is higher than that disclosed by the HRA. For example if an authority charges rent of £25 a week on a property that "costs" the HRA £30 a week, then the subsidy shown in the HRA is £5 a week. But imagine that the price of a similar house in the private sector was £45 a week. Then the true subsidy would be £20 a week (£45 − £25), representing an HRA subsidy of £5 a week and lost opportunity for income to the local authority of a further £15 a week.

Housing services provided for the private sector

Housing authorities are seen primarily as providers of council houses. They also have an important role to play in providing assistance to the private sector through capital grants and loans. This role is likely to become increasingly important as the authorities move closer towards their new role of enablers rather than providers of housing services. Whereas the expense of running the council house service after 1990 will not be a charge on the local taxpayers aid to the private sector remains an expense to general funds.

Net revenue costs of housing services to the private sector

'Old' system
The old system of housing grants given by local authorities to the private sector was described in detail in Chapter 5. There were no capital grants generally available from the Government to help local authorities to make these payments and local authorities borrowed money to cover the cash outflow. The Government gave the local authorities annual grants to cover some of the costs attributable to the schemes as follows:
— Slum Clearance Subsidy was given to housing authorities making an annual loss on approved slum clearance projects. The grant was payable on each year's losses for a maximum of 15 years at a rate of 75% of the net loss.
— Environmental Improvements Grants were available on works carried out in General Improvement and Housing Action Areas. The grant payable was equal to 50% of the debt charges for twenty years on approved schemes, subject to a maximum of £400 times the number of dwellings in the area.
— House Renovation Grants, as described in Chapter 5, included grants for improvement and repairs, intermediate grants and special grants. The Government paid a subsidy of 90% on

the grants paid in 'priority cases' and 75% on other cases. The subsidy rate applied to 20 years of debt charges on the money borrowed to finance the original grants.

— Home Insulation schemes offered grants to owner/occupiers under local approved schemes. The grants were 100% funded by the government which might make an annual contribution towards the cost of running the scheme.

The housing authority paid the difference between the cost of provision of its housing services to the private sector and the contribution made by the Government from the general funds.

"New" system

The new system of renovation grants and renewal areas as set out in the Local Government and Housing Act 1989 are described in Chapter 5. Capital expenditure in these areas is to be partly met by Government capital grants. The rest of the expenditure will be met from other funds of the local authority. The Act also proposes that in the case of slum clearance if the authority makes a surplus the Secretary of State may require that some of it be paid to him, with interest.

General funds available to pay the net revenue costs of the provision of housing services to the private sector

General funds are used to pay for services available to all the people living in a local authority area rather than just those who are council tenants. The main sources of these funds are taxes paid by the residents of the district and the grants paid by the Government to support spending on behalf of those residents. The Local Government Finance Act 1988 prepared the way for radical changes in the local government finance system from 1990/91. Domestic rates will be replaced by the community charge and the Rate Support Grant by the Revenue Support Grant.

From the local taxpayer: The "old" system

Local authorities and the government are the only bodies in the United Kingdom with the power to levy taxes. The government levies a variety of taxes, Income Tax, VAT, Corporation Tax on company profits and so on. Local authorities levy one tax, under the old system this was the rates. Rates were a tax on property. Each property liable for rating was given a 'rateable value' based on its expected rental value in a free market. This rateable value was the amount on which the tax to be paid by the occupier of the property was based.

The tax base of a local authority was the total rateable value of the rateable property in its area, but not all property in the area was rated, the major exceptions being agricultural land and some crown properties. Occupiers of rateable properties were required to pay rates on their properties. The amount the occupier was liable to pay in rates was:

$$\text{The rateable value of the property} \times \text{The rate in the £ levied by the local taxing authority}$$

The 'rate in the pound' was the tax rate charged by the local authority, determined by the authority's need to collect enough income to pay its bills plus, in the case of a district council, an additional amount required by the County Council. Most local authorities were allowed to levy any rate the Council, as representatives of the inhabitants of the area, recommended. A few authorities were required to keep their rate levy within a maximum rate specified by the Government. This system of 'rate capping' was introduced in 1984 to allow the Government more detailed control over the spending of local authorities which did not respond to the control measures built into the Block Grant mechanism (see below).

Rates were an old tax, developing from the liability placed on local inhabitants to pay rates towards costs incurred under the Poor Relief Act of 1601. They were cheap to collect and difficult to evade, it is much easier to lie about personal income levels than occupancy of property. However compared to a modern tax such as income tax the rating system did have several unattractive properties. These were:

(a) The tax base was inelastic. The tax base for income tax is personal incomes and these rise with inflation. The government can therefore, in periods of inflation, collect more money to pay for its rising expenditure without increasing the rate of income tax. Rateable values, once calculated, seldom changed. If the local authority wished to increase its income to meet rising costs it had to increase the tax rate. This gave rates a much higher profile than income tax.

(b) Rates were a regressive tax. This means that they bore more heavily on the poor than on the rich, unlike income tax which, in theory bears equally on all payers. The burden rates could place on the low income groups were reduced in several ways including the following:

  i Government grants paid to local authorities reduced the need for the local authority to raise rates to pay for their services. These grants included the Domestic Rate Relief grant which reduces the burden on domestic ratepayers.

  ii Rate rebates reduced the rate bills of low income households. The rebates were means-tested and operated in the same way as rent rebates.

The liability to pay rates was based on rateable value which related to property value. In the early 20th century, this was considered to be appropriate as most of the services provided by local authorities were associated with property and rates, although a tax, could be considered as a payment for services rendered. Since then local authorities have lost many of their powers to provide services associated with properties and now provide most of their services for people. The link between the amount of rates paid and the services received is much weaker than before and rates are now seen much more clearly as a tax with an inadequate and outmoded tax base.

A criticism aimed at the rating system by the Government was that it did not match those who vote for services with those who pay for them. There are 35 million electors in England and Wales and 18 million of them paid rates. There were some 17 million local electors who could, in theory, vote for extravagant service provision without having to face the prospect of paying towards the cost of such provision.

It was also argued that business people paying rates on commercial properties were subject to taxation without representation. Occupiers of commercial properties could only vote in the election of the Council that determined the rates they paid on their commercial property if they also lived in the area. In 1984/85 17% of local government income in England was raised from non-domestic rates compared with 11% from domestic rates.

From the government
The Government contributed to the costs of running local authority services not aided by specific grants through the Rate Support Grant. This consisted of two elements:

— Domestic Rate Relief was paid to all authorities in England at a rate such that domestic rate payers paid 18.5p in the £ less in rates than commercial ratepayers.
— The 'Block Grant' was given in support of local authority expenditure less specific grants, this was termed 'total expenditure'. The amount of grant payable for a year was calculated for each authority according to the following formula:

$$\text{Block Grant} = \text{Total Expenditure} - \text{Local Contribution}$$

where the 'local contribution' is the amount the government thinks the authority should be raising from local taxation.

The basic formula shown above, supported by a number of sub formula, was used to distribute the total grant available between all local authorities. These sub formulae varied each year and often within each year. The grant was intended to equalise needs and resources, that is the formula was to be constructed in such a way as to compensate for the fact that not all authorities were faced with the same demand for services or had the same resources to meet the demand. The distribution methods described here only applied to England.

Each local authority was assessed according to its need to spend to provide a common standard of services. The need for authorities in England to spend money on service provision was expressed by the Government, after negotiations with local authorities, as a national Grant Related Expenditure (GRE). This national GRE was made up of eight service GREs, one of which was for housing. These national

GREs were then shared out to authorities using up to 64 indicators of need. The GRE for an authority was the sum of the individual service assessments of need and was unique to that authority.

In theory, an authority's GRE represented a level of expenditure that the Government would wish the authority to use as a spending target, any authority spending below GRE should be encouraged to increase expenditure and bring its services up to the nationally accepted standard, and any authority spending above GRE should be discouraged from doing so. The discouragement to high spenders was reduced grant. All formulae used since 1980 delivered this, more generous grants for levels of expenditure up to slightly above GRE and then less generous grants for spending above that level.

The first 'Block Grant' settlements provided 'open-ended grants'. The more local authorities spent, the more grant had to be made available. At a time when the Government was becoming increasingly interested in controlling local government expenditure this was not acceptable. Block grant settlements became progressively less generous as the Government strove to use the mechanism to control local authority revenue spending. Two major changes in emphasis were introduced.

Firstly, in 1981/82 the Government introduced 'targets' for each local authority. These targets, which were based on past spending patterns, were used in addition to GREs. Some authorities had targets above GRE and some below. Authorities whose spending exceeded target were subject to grant penalties. This meant that they lost grant progressively for spending over target and, if the overspending was sufficient, lost grant altogether. Some authorities had targets that were less than GRE and lost grant if they tried to spend up to the level of what had originally been considered necessary expenditure.

Secondly, the Government introduced negative grants for some authorities at certain levels of expenditure. This meant that an authority might go on receiving grant up to a little above GRE and then any spending after that point would be punished by the gradual withdrawal of grant until the authority eventually lost grant altogether. This method had the advantage of providing a greater incentive to authorities to curtail their expenditure and of allowing the Government to 'close-end' the grant. Extra local authority spending did not automatically generate extra grant. The Government also ensured that only the planned amount of grant for a year was distributed by changing the sub formulae during the year to fine tune the distribution.

The operation of targets brought the Block Grant system into disrepute, souring the already strained relationships between the Government and the local authorities, and targets were withdrawn in 1986. The old system then returned to the use of GREs as the desirable level of spending but the grant curve for most authorities was negative at all but very low levels of expenditure. In practice this meant that at the very low levels of expenditure the grant payable was equal to the total expenditure. At higher spending levels the grant was less than total expenditure and the more the authority spent, the less grant it got. Loss of grant was less severe for expenditure just above GRE, but after that point the grant loss was more severe until the authority loses its entitlement to grant altogether.

The Block Grant system has been heavily criticised by local government, the Audit Commission and many other bodies involved in local government finance. The main areas of criticism were as follows:

— The formula was so complex, with over 60 indicators of need and complicated safety nets to prevent wide fluctuations in grant entitlement, that very few people understood it.

— Because of the regular changes in the formulae individual local authorities could not predict with any certainty how much Block Grant they would receive in a year until the final adjustment was made to the formulae. The authorities were not told what their grant entitlement would be in the future. This uncertainty, which was probably the major fault of the system, makes it impossible for local authorities to plan more than one year at a time.

— The equalisation of resources was based on the rating system. This means that the system equalised to low rateable values rather than the individuals ability to pay. This did not target resources at low income groups.

Criticisms were also levied at the combined effect of rates and rate support grant. The Government considers that the major indicator of an authority's spending should be its tax demand, that if the tax demand goes up this should indicate a higher level of spending. Local authorities levied rates to make up the difference between expenditure and the income generated from charges and government grants. If the main government grant fluctuated then so would the rate levy. So, in theory, an authority could have hidden increased spending behind a fortuitous grant gain without having to signal this to the electorate through a rate increase.

Proposed changes to the grant

— The abolition of the Domestic Rate Relief Grant, as domestic rates are to be replaced by the community charge this grant is no longer relevant.

— The Government has decided that as part of its programme for reforming the local government finance system that the Block Grant will be replaced by a Revenue Support Grant. The new grant is expected to be based on GREs calculated using about 10 indicators, including one for each major service. The amount of the grant payable to each authority would be fixed at the start of the year and would not alter subsequently.

The Government intends to announce each year its plans for local authority grants for the forthcoming financial year and the two years after that. This should allow local authorities to plan for the future with greater confidence than was possible before.

The "new" taxation system. The Government has replaced the rates charged to householders by a community charge levied on the adult population in their area, thus most of those entitled to vote in local government elections will have to contribute to the costs of services they vote for. The community charge will be a flat rate charge although some categories of voters, such as students, will only pay 20% of the charge and some, such as inmates of H.M. Prisons and long stay patients in hospitals will be exempt. Charge payers with low incomes will receive assistance through a community charge benefit scheme.

The old system of levying rates on commercial property continues as a uniform rating system with the rate in the pound determined nationally. This poundage will be indexed in line with inflation. Commercial rates now become a national tax automatically enfranchising the ratepayers. The proceeds of the business rate will be paid into a pool maintained by the government and paid out to local authorities on a per capita basis.

The effects of these changes will be that the resources available to each authority from non-domestic rates and the community charge will depend only on the number of adult residents in its area.

The new grant to support the community charge is called the 'Revenue Support Grant' and like the new tax system aims to be simpler and more easily understood than its predecessor. The reason that the Block Grant formula was so complicated was that it was required to calculate the grant payable at any level of spending. The new revenue support grant formula is only required to return one answer, the grant for the year. The grant will be paid to district authorities and will support all expenditure in the area, both at district and county level. Although the precise formula for the new grant has not been published it is expected that grant payable will equal:

Standard expenditure

−

local contribution

−

contribution from national non domestic rates pool

Where 'standard expenditure' is the amount the Government wants the local authorities in the area to spend. This is equivalent to the old GRE and is calculated in a similar way but using fewer indicators of need.

'Local contribution' is the tax raised by levying a nationally determined standard community charge in the area.

The 'contribution from the national non domestic rates pool' is the payment made to local authorities from this pool distributed in proportion to the adult population in the area.

These figures can all be expressed in £ per head of adult population and used to compare the actual expenditure of local authorities on the services provided in the area with the government standard.

For example – in District A the Government considers that expenditure per adult should be £700, the nationally determined standard community charge will be £250 and the amount that all local authorities will receive from the national non domestic rates pool will be £150 per adult. The Revenue Support Grant payable will be £(700 − 250 − 150), £300 per adult. The district and county may decide that the needs of the area can be satisfied by spending £680 per adult and raising a community charge of £30 for the district and £200 for the county. This information will be shown on the community charge demand and chargepayers will be able to make comparisons as shown in Figure 3.8.6.

	£ per adult Standard	£ per adult Actual
Net expenditure	700	680
Financed by		
Revenue Support Grant	300	300
National non domestic rates pool	150	150
Community Charge	250	230
	700	680

Figure 3.8.6

In this case the community charge demand for District A will clearly show that their spending is within Government guidelines.

This system can also be used to show that authorities are spending more than Government guidelines. For example see Figure 3.8.7 to see how the community charge levied by District B in the same year might be displayed on its community charge demand as:

	£ per adult Standard	£ per adult Actual
Net expenditure	650	690
Financed by		
Revenue Support Grant	250	250
National non domestic rates pool	150	150
Community Charge	250	290
	650	690

Figure 3.8.7

In this case the standard expenditure per adult determined by the Government is £50 less than for District A resulting in a Revenue Support Grant payment to District B of £50 per adult less than that awarded to District A. District B and its county have however decided that the Government standard is inadequate and are prepared to fund the extra expenditure by levying a community charge greater than the nationally determined standard. The chargepayers are made aware of this decision through the information provided on the community charge demand.

The Treasury claims that the result of the new arrangements will be to ensure that each pound per adult more or less that the authority spends will add to or reduce community charge bills by one pound.

The 35 million elector/chargepayers will exercise control through the ballot box.

The degree of local accountability that the new system brings to the operation of the local government finance system is seen by the Government as being strong enough to remove the need for the attempt to control spending through the Block Grant system.

Criticisms of the new finance system
The community charge has been severely criticised for having many of the faults of the rating system. It provides local government with yet another inelastic tax base and the tax is clearly regressive. It also has few of the virtues of the rating system, it is likely to be four or five times as expensive to collect as rates and much easier to evade. It is claimed that the new system will deliver, if anything, less money to local authorities than the old and since housing services must compete for funds with other services, less money to housing.

Revenue budgeting – a final word

Most local authority budgets are prepared on an incremental basis. This means that the starting point for estimating the income and expenditure for next year is the most up to date estimate for spending in the current year. Local authorities prepare their annual budgets in the period September to February before the start of the year. At this time the actual spending for the first half of the current year is known and a fairly accurate estimate of the full year expenditure can be made. This estimate for the current year forms the basis of the calculations of next years budget which is calculated as:

Estimate for current year
+
Revenue cost of the capital programme for next year
+
Cost of new revenue schemes to start next year
–
Cost of schemes dropping out next year

The estimate will usually be prepared at November, current year, prices. A contingency fund will be set aside to pay for price increases.

In preparing the HRA budget the authority will, after 1990, have to ensure that sufficient rent income is collected to avoid a deficit. The rent levels set should be sufficiently high so that the income collected when added to the specific grant income will cover all expenditure and bad debts.

Once the budget is set it becomes the financial plan of the authority and every effort should be made to keep to it. The total expenditure and income should be broken down into budget centres with one person, the budgetholder responsible for controlling spending or the level of income. The budget centre may be increased to take account of inflation during the year, this increase would be vired from the contingency reserve. The actual expenditure and income will be recorded and should be compared with the estimates. Any serious variance should be questioned and the budgetholder required to answer for it and if found to be negligent, reprimanded.

It is useful to be able to prepare revenue budgets for several years at a time, establishing a rolling programme. In recent years local authorities have been prevented from doing this because they could not be certain, sometimes even during a financial year, of the amount of money they would receive from government grants or how much they would be allowed to spend on capital schemes. Most of the barriers to longer term planning presented by the Government's failures in these areas are about to be removed and in future local authorities should be able to make reasonably reliable medium term revenue plans.

Audit of local authorities

So far the chapters on local authority housing have concentrated on the financing of the service and the recording of the financial transactions through the accounting system and the use of budgets to define and control expenditure. The accounting system presents a detailed record of the financial decisions taken and implemented by the council and this record is used as a management document to inform future policy decisions. It is also a record of the use of the authorities most vulnerable asset, cash. Such an important record must be checked and verified and this function is carried out by accountants responsible for auditing the accounts. Local authorities employ two distinct groups of auditors:

— internal auditors, who work for the authority, and
— external auditors, independent of the authority.

External audit
The external auditor to a local authority is appointed by the Audit Commission, a body of government appointees, established in 1982. The auditor appointed can be member of the staff of the Commission, that is a member of the District Audit Service, or a partner in a private firm of accountants. The auditor and his/her staff will work in the offices of the local authority for the period of the audit.

The external auditor is responsible for checking that the annual accounts of the local authority have been prepared in accordance with statute and best accounting practice. Particular attention will be paid to accounts containing information used in grant claims. The auditor has access to all the documents of the authority and the power to question individuals.

After completing the audit the auditor has to give a certificate and an opinion on the accounts. Any report he makes to the local authority is also sent to the Audit Commission. If the auditor uncovers illegal expenditure or a failure to collect income the persons involved may be taken to court and, if found guilty of an offence fined or, in the case of a member of the council, disqualified from membership of the council for a specified period.

Internal audit
In local authorities internal audit is the responsibility of the Chief Financial Officer. Internal audit is concerned with ensuring that no fraud or misrepresentation of accounts occur and of developing management systems that discourage these crimes. For example, a system that would discourage theft of housing rent income by the officers of the council could include the following features:
— The calculation of housing rents and their notification to tenants would not be carried out by officers involved in rent collecting.
— All tenants would be given a rent book showing clearly their liability to the council.
— Non-cash payment should be encouraged. Cheques, standing orders, direct debit etc are less attractive to thieves than coins and notes.
— Tenants to be offered the choice of payment locations.

The internal auditors are not only concerned with setting up financial management systems but also in maintaining them. They will be interested in ensuring that the systems are used and have not been replaced by an individual's own-design system. They will also be involved in adapting existing systems to deal with changing circumstances.

An important duty of the internal audit section is to liaise with the external auditors to prevent duplication of effort. The external auditor may choose not to run detailed checks in areas already covered by internal audit.

Value for money audits
The accounts of local authorities are concerned with recording expenditure and income not with calculating the success or otherwise of the financial transactions in meeting the objectives of the authority.

For example, an authority decides to spend an average of £2,000 per dwelling on renovating 30% of its housing stock in order to extend the useful life of that stock by an average of 15 years. At the end of the year the council wishes to know if the money was spent to best advantage.

The information in the HRA will tell the council whether or not the money was spent. The other information needed, the statistics of work done, the opinions about increased useful life and the alternative use of the money, will have to come from other sources. One way of dealing with all this information is by a Value for Money (VFM) audit which can be carried out by members of the internal audit staff who will assess the expenditure in terms of economy, efficiency and effectiveness.

At a national level, the Audit Commission is empowered to undertake or promote studies designed to enable it to make recommendations for improving economy, efficiency and effectiveness in the provision of local authority services and for improving the financial or other management of local authorities. The Commission have recently published three reports of interest to housing students. In 1986 they published a pair of reports on 'Managing the Crisis in Council Housing' and 'Improving Council House Maintenance' and in 1989 'Housing the Homeless – the local authority role'. The Commission have also published a number of reports on other services.

Conclusion

This book has been written at a time when the role of local government as a provider of services is being questioned, its services eroded and its finances being reformed. The changes required by the Local Government Finance Act 1988, the two consultation papers published in 1988, the Housing Act 1988 and the Local Government and Housing Act 1989 will ensure that local authority housing finance in the 1990s will operate under quite different rules to those prevailing in 1989.